Hard Target

Decreasing the opportunity for crime by becoming a Guardian

WARNING

The armed and unarmed techniques described in this book are by nature intended to cause injury and are extremely dangerous. They are discussed to give you the confidence that you can defend yourself in any circumstance and against any opponent. However, this book cannot replace training with a proper self-defense or NRA instructor. The use of force described in this book is for information purposes only. Neither the author nor the publisher assumes any responsibility for the use or misuse of information contained in this book.

ACKNOWLEDGEMENTS

I would like to thank Lt. Randy Webb for the opportunity he gave me to learn to prevent crime by going outside of traditional policing.

I also have to acknowledge Dr. Pam Wilcox, Dr. John Eck, and Dr. Robin Engel who helped expand my understanding of both policing and crime prevention.

I also bow to Nidan Christopher Beard, Godan Mark Gregory, and Shihan Greg Heeg for the dozens of bruises and many years of training in Budo-taijutsu. I was blessed to know such gentle men that also found great joy in dropping others on their heads.

My wife, Pamela, who supported me through the years of working the nightshift with no idea if her husband would come home in the morning, allowing me the hours spent each week training at the dojo to increase the chances that I would come home, and dealing with the stress of watching me struggle with statistics to earn a Masters Degree in Criminal Justice. Thanks for the years of support and understanding.

To my daughter, Trinity Grace, who proved to be the greatest blessing in life that I never knew I needed. I pray you grow to be a guardian for the next generation.

HARD TARGET

The local news is a great confirmation of just how dangerous the world is. Add in a dose of national news and before you know it you feel like it's not safe to leave the house. A constant bombardment of active shootings, riots and terrorism makes you unsure if locking the doors and staying home is any safer.

The news, like drama, is driven by conflict and is marinated with a fair amount of excitement. News producers are driven to have the highest ratings. That means that the violence is reported first with facts as unnecessary filler. Perhaps you've heard of police not wanting to make comments to the media. Much of that is based on the knowledge that no matter what is said, it will end up on the television edited and spun out of context. Recognize that truth when you hear how bad crime is in your community.

The simple fact is violence has been decreasing nationally over the past two decades. This can be confirmed by looking up both Universal Crime Reports and the National Crime Survey online. However, an increase of mass killings and school shootings has gone from none in the idyllic 1950s to roughly 6 a year in the 2000s and doubling that for the past several years. These events become the stories that play in continuous loops on 24-hour news channels as they feed a morbid fascination for producers and audiences alike, spurring debates over gun control and mental health.

Most books on personal security push the idea that it is a dangerous world out there. The truth is the danger is generally only in very specific places. If you can minimize your time in such locations, your chances of being victimized are greatly diminished. As we will see, the single best way to win a fight is to avoid the conflict.

The first goal of this book is to reassure you that crime, and violent crime in particular, is not as bad as the news would make you believe. Much of the crime that is seen is limited to a few individuals and it is the same few people that tend to be the victims. By simply following some common sense approaches you can substantially decrease your odds of victimization. The second focus of the book is to give you the skills necessary to protect yourself and win if things turn bad.

SOME BASIC FACTS ON CRIME

The nightly news starts off with one person shot and 3 people injured. It seems to be a nightly refrain if you live anywhere near a major metropolitan area. The underlying theme is that your city is dangerous and that crime can happen to anyone at any time.

That might be true, but it's highly unlikely. Sherman in 1989 did a study of Minneapolis, Minnesota and found that only about 3 percent of locations in the city accounted for about 50% of all the violent crimes. In the same year, Eck and Spelman found a similar 10% of locations accounting for more than 60% of crime. Over the past 30 years this type of finding has become fairly common knowledge in crime science. Crime is rarely widespread throughout a neighborhood; it's almost always concentrated to only a handful of places within those neighborhoods (Braga, Papachristos & Hureau, 2012). Knowing these simple facts reveals that by simply avoiding a small number of high crime locations known as 'hot spots', you are likely to decrease your odds of being a victim of crime by 50% to 60%.

Most people assume that certain locations are expected to be more dangerous just by the nature of the business. Convenient stores, bars, and nightclubs are those sort of places that mom always warned you about. But it's not necessarily the type of location; it's more directly related to the specific location. There is something about the layout or management of specific locations that directly influences behavior, causing people to become violent or criminal. As an example, it's well accepted that bars are dangerous places where random fights are likely to break out due to alcohol. However, a study of all the bars in Cincinnati found that only 20% accounted for 75% of the violent crimes (Madenson & Eck, 2008). This makes it clear that it's not the type of business, but something unique about certain businesses that make them more likely to draw crime.

It's not just locations that lead to more crime, but there are certain people that are also likely to be repeat victims. Farrell and Pease conducted a study in 1993 that found that 4% of victims suffer more than 44% of victimizations. That indicates that there is something that people who are victimized repeatedly do that makes them easier targets for crime. They are most likely involved in a relationship with a significant other that consistently attacks them. The may also do something that makes them an easy target for crime such as engaging in criminal conduct themselves or by choosing to return time and time again to high crime locations.

What this makes clear is that many people that become victims are making decisions that make it easier for others to take advantage of them, or are engaging in behavior that is likely to be criminal. The odds of the average person becoming a victim of violent crime are extremely low, largely because so few people engage in violent behavior. Robin Engel's research Cincinnati's Initiative to Reduce Violence (CIRV) found that less than .03% of the population accounted for 75% of the violence in the city. Similarly, the National Gang Center shows that gang-related murders make up 12% of the reported homicides with more than two thirds occurring in cities with a population greater than 100,000. In major cities like Chicago and Los Angeles, nearly half of all homicides are related to gang violence. Gang violence makes up a significant amount of the homicides reported each year, with most of it concentrated in the largest cities. Within those cities, the areas of violence tend to be highly localized to only a few city blocks.

What researchers are consistently finding is that only a very small percentage of locations account for most of the violent crime. In addition, only a small percentage of people in society are extremely violent and only a very small number of people are consistently the victims of crime.

Across studies, roughly 5% of people will cause half of all reported crime, less than 5% of people will be victims, and of those, many will be victimized repeatedly. In addition, less than 5% of locations are high crime locations. This concentration is not peculiar to crime and disorder, but is practically a universal law (Bak, 1999).

Economist Vilfredo Pareto was the first to explain this phenomenon when he recognized that 80% of the land was owned by only 20% of the population. Pareto's Law is consistent across almost all aspects of life. Only a small portion of the earth's surface holds the majority of life on earth. Only a small amount of earthquakes cause most of the earthquake damage. A very small number of people hold most of the world's wealth (Forst et al., 1982; Forst et al., 1977). In fact, the richest 85 people in the world have more wealth than the poorest 3.5 billion combined. Pareto's Law has become known as the 80-20 rule where 20% of some things are responsible for 80% of the outcomes (Kock, 1999). Although this figure varies slightly, the consistent finding is that a small percentage of factors cause a large percentage of the results (Eck & Clarke, 2007). Crime and violence are bound by this same pattern, as are most other things in life.

The nightly news certainly paints a far grimmer picture of the world, but once you see the facts, the likelihood of being the victim of a violent crime comes more into perspective. It can happen, but it is most likely to happen in only a few places and to those that are already engaging in a risky lifestyle.

What that means is much of crime prevention is up to you. It really isn't the role of the police. Police serve the purpose of investigating crime and in order maintenance. Although most of us feel that the police prevent crime, they only have a minor deterrent effect. People that engage in a criminal lifestyle understand that the odds of being caught by the police are slim. The odds of serving any serious time for a crime is even less. If you only get caught in a crime once in a hundred times, aren't those pretty good odds?

The odds of the policing catching a criminal in the act by randomly driving up on a crime in progress or by rapid response to a call for service are less than 3%. Rapid response to crime is unnecessary in 75% of crimes reported because by the time a crime is recognized the suspect is long since gone (Spelman and Brown, 1974). John Eck reviewed research on community problem oriented policing going back through the 1970s, finding repeatedly that police patrolling neighborhoods does not decrease crime and having the police respond quickly to calls for service does not reduce crime.

Part of the problem of catching a criminal in the act is that there is an average delay of 2 minutes from when a person sees a crime to determine if they should call the police. All too frequently, the police are usually the second person a witness calls after they call their best friend. It's usually the friend that tells them to call the police. The witness may be in such a state of shock that they are trying to determine if an event warrants calling the police, or if they are simply overreacting to what they saw (Kelling, et al, 1974).

This makes it clear that randomly trying to attack crime from traditional policing will do little to reduce it. Most locations simply won't experience a significant amount of crime. As Dr. Carl Klockars says, "It makes about as much sense to have police patrol routinely in cars to fight crime as it does to have firemen patrol routinely in fire trucks to fight fire." Instead, if we focus patrols on those specific numbers of repeat offenders, victims, and places we can make a dent in half of all crime. Unfortunately, most Police and Sheriff's departments don't have the knowledge or the manpower to pull off such preventative patrols and they remain locked in a dated philosophy of dealing with crime through investigation and arrest.

Although much of CBS's line-up involves the title CSI, very few crimes are actually solved through follow up investigations. It is only those high profile crimes such as murder, where investigations lead to arrests. Most investigations of common crimes do not lead to an arrest, and those that do, don't reduce crime. In fact, only about twenty-one percent of reported index crimes are solved through arrest. Those that lead to an arrest only prevent additional crime for the time the criminal is incarcerated. Once released, a criminal will simply return to the lifestyle he knows.

Increasing arrests do not lead to a significant reduction in crime. Much of the time, zero tolerance approaches by the police only erodes police effectiveness as the public begins to question their actions. The police begin to be seen as heavy-handed tools of the state and the people refuse to help. In addition, arrests only work on people that have something to lose. If you are tied to the community with a good paying job and a family an arrest can be devastating to your life. But if you live on the fringe of society with very few friends and no job to speak of, what do you have to lose if you spend a couple of days in jail? In reality, it's that fringe of society where most criminals exist. For these people, jail time is simply part of life and only goes to build their street cred.

Even the idea of adding additional officers is unlikely to significantly reduce crime. After you account for three shifts, off days and vacations most departments can only expect one or two more officers at best per shift at a district or precinct level. This was summarized by Levine in a 1975 study that found, "It is tempting for government leaders to add more police: it is intuitively sensible solution to an unrelenting problem. The sad fact is, that they receive a false sense of security."

The way police follow up with crime is largely determined by the amount of crime that exists in its jurisdiction. A small town might be able to dedicate time to investigate a burglary with little evidence. In a major city, dealing with multiple shootings, such an event may only be a report with almost no investigation.

When you see the truth about policing, relying on the police to stop crime from happening is just not very likely. However, the media portrays police work in a way that even the police buy into the image of preventing crime. The simple fact is that only 3% to 5% of crimes are solved by an arrest at the scene. When you consider that those figures include domestic violence where both sides are present, you see how unlikely that is. Crime simply happens too quickly for the police to arrive in time to prevent most events.

What you need to understand is that if a crime happens you have to act as your own first responder. It's up to you to determine what you are willing and capable of doing in response to a crime. If you fall and break your leg, you recognize that the ambulance will take time to get there. However, we tend not to have a similar understanding of crime. If you are attacked you expect the police to immediately respond. In truth, it may take several minutes for help to arrive, and that assumes someone calls as the crime is occurring. If a gun is involved, it is likely the police will stage, waiting for enough manpower before they roll in to confront the threat. That means the majority of the time, by the time the police arrive, they are investigating a crime, not preventing it.

This book is designed to make you aware of how criminals tend to think, the locations and victims they tend to favor, and what you can do to avoid being victimized or win if it does happen.

ROUTINE ACTIVITIES THEORY

For almost two centuries criminologists have tried to determine what makes certain people into criminals. For years, the dominant thought was that criminals were biologically presupposed to crime. Criminals were less evolved and by studying their physical characteristics it was possible to determine their tendency towards deviant behavior.

This was followed by the idea that outside forces from society either forced people into crime or tended to draw them into crime. In truth, each new theory revealed some reality as to why certain crimes occurred, but they never revealed the single thing that would prevent crime. These multiple conflicting theories require long-term and large social change, but little evidence of how they could be put into practice.

Criminology looks at the criminal and thinks in terms of making national, city level, or neighborhood changes to decrease crime by rehabilitating the criminal. However, in the 1970s a new approach developed called crime science. Crime science wasn't concerned about understanding and changing criminals, but was based on eliminating opportunity. Rather than changing society at large it attempted to understand crime at a far more localized level such as a block, or even a single address.

In 1979 two researchers developed the idea that the routine activities of victims and criminals shape crime opportunities. For any crime to occur three conditions for crime have to be met: A motivated offender has to stumble upon a suitable victim in an area that lacks a capable guardian. This can occur anywhere, but certain areas are more conducive to crime.

This theory of crime has become one of the most tested over the past couple of decades. It's really a theory of victimization and not of offenders. It doesn't explain, or care, why people are driven to crime. It doesn't try to explain an offender's motivation. It doesn't care if mommy didn't love him enough or that society wasn't fair. It merely shows why crime is more likely to occur in some situations. Once you understand this basic concept, you can begin to see where crime is likely to happen and how you might be able to prevent it before it does.

Cohen and Felson (1979) developed the idea of routine activities theory after witnessing a sharp increase in crime during the 60's and 70's, despite improvements in living conditions of the urban poor. They saw that there were major changes in the daily routine of the average American following the World War II era that led to an increase in possible victimization. As an example, as more women entered the workforce, homes were left vacant during the day, both increasing the risk of homes being burglarized during the day and of women being victimized by being away from the safety of the home. Cohen and Felson believed that the routines of the modern lifestyle made the likelihood of a willing offender coming into contact with an appealing target without a capable guardian far more likely.

Cohen and Felson's insight allows for an effective way of personal crime prevention. By looking at specific factors you have the ability to make targets less suitable. Most criminological theories required macro solutions that involve changing the behavior of criminals and society. That type of change doesn't happen overnight and there's no guarantee that they will work even after years of effort and billions of dollars spent. Such efforts require massive changes that only governments can enact.

However, routine activities can be implemented down to the individual, home, or the business. Knowing that you can take specific actions to decrease your perceived ease of victimization puts you in control over what might happen to you, not government agencies.

On college campuses, routine activities theory finds a suitable proving ground. Colleges are filled with those in their late teens and early twenties who are the people most likely to be both the victims and perpetrators of criminal behavior (NCVS, 1993). Most live in multi-unit dorms or apartment buildings, frequently with a roommate that they may only know in passing. If they live in an all-male dorm, they are much more likely to be victimized, as they are living with the demographic most likely to be offenders. Most students view both their rooms and the college campus as safe locations, often leaving doors unlocked and valuable items unattended (Fisher, et al. 1998). IPads, iPhones, and laptops are small, high value items that all too often are left unguarded, if only for a moment, making for tempting bait for a willing thief.

College campuses are learning grounds. Unfortunately, students are often learning what their blood alcohol level is before blacking out. This behavior leads many students to be victims of violence or sexual assault. Fisher's study found that the unique routines of college students led nearly a third of his sample to be victims of some type of crime during their academic year.

Like drinking, many college students begin to experiment with marijuana. Mustaine and Tewksbury (1998) found that those that smoked marijuana were nearly two and half times more likely to be theft victims than those that did not. They are likely to be targeted, as their own criminal behavior makes them unwilling to report a crime that might get them into trouble. Mustaine and Tewksbury found that much of **what leads to victimization of college students is largely based on where they are and what they do while they are there that makes them targets.**

College students perceive the university surrounding as a protected environment, when in reality, college campuses are filled with the demographic age most likely to engage in risky and criminal behavior. By letting down their guard and experimenting with drugs and alcohol, many students routinely make themselves attractive targets to an offender looking for an easy mark.

In essence, we make ourselves victims. We become complacent in our daily lives and become disconnected to our environment. This is not to take responsibility off of the criminal. They are still guilty for their actions. However, we give them opportunity to commit a crime. If we can eliminate the opportunity, we can decrease the odds of being victimized.

To decrease opportunity for crime we have to affect the criminal, victim, or the location in some way. Our issue is that we don't always know who our victims and offenders will be. However, we can largely predict where they are likely to meet because most offenders will operate under rational choice, even if their rational thoughts are tempered with a fair amount of alcohol or peer pressure (Clark & Cornish, 1985). Criminals naturally seek out certain locations that make their risk of getting caught significantly less. These areas generally have environmental factors that benefit crime such as areas to hide or quick escape routes where no one provides any guardianship.

RATIONAL CHOICE THEORY

Placing a gun against the head of a stranger for money hardly seems the act of a rational person. Rational people know that money is earned through labor or is the result of creative work. It does not come from the barrel of a gun. However, to the person committing the robbery, the steps necessary to accomplish their goal without getting caught or killed are deliberate and built on quite rational and logical decisions.

In 1985 Clarke and Cornish developed the idea that criminals do not act randomly, but make rational decisions when planning and executing crimes. These actions may only be rational to themselves, as they are frequently driven by drugs, alcohol, and limited information. Despite these influences, **criminals consistently look for easy targets, relatively low risk, and high reward**. Clarke and Cornish created a framework to understand this rational approach to crime by offenders. They identified several stages criminals go through to become involved in crime. They called these the initial involvement phase, the criminal event itself, continuance in the criminal behavior, and desistance from crime. This framework shows us the large and small decisions that criminals go through before engaging in crime.

In the initial involvement stage a person begins to prepare himself for criminal activity. The fledgling offender begins to set in his mind that if circumstances were right he would commit a crime to provide himself with a perceived need of money, sex, or excitement. The offender calculates that legal alternatives are less effective or more difficult at meeting his basic needs. After filtering through his own life experiences and moral code he determines just what he is willing to do to get what he wants.

The second component of this stage is a chance opportunity that presents itself to the offender. A person with a strong moral code would see a backpack left unattended and think that someone is being naïve to leave it unattended, but he or she would never commit the act of taking it. Their upbringing simply would not allow it. But a backpack left out to someone who has already prepared himself to commit a criminal act will immediately be seen as an easy opportunity. If the offender is with others urging him to act, he is more likely to spring at the opportunity.

This applies equally well to a violent crime. A person walking alone down a side street, engrossed in a Twitter conversation on his iPhone, unwittingly reveals himself as an easy target. The criminal, knowing that the iPhone holds value and is easily taken from someone unaware of his surroundings, suddenly is presented a quick solution to his financial problems.

This leads the offender directly into the criminal event itself. The offender has gauged the opportunity that is in front of him and determines the risks inherent in taking an item. Is anyone nearby? Is he being baited? How quickly can I exit the area without drawing attention? Are there other items that would be easier to take? The offender determines if an item has value and if so, can it be rapidly converted into cash? **All decisions are weighed to determine if this target is both convenient and poses a limited risk.**

The offender may wait and watch for the right moment to act, or the decision to act can be made in a matter of seconds. Ultimately, **the offender will act if he perceives the potential of meeting his needs**

by committing the crime exceeds whatever risk he may encounter. This decision may also be fueled by a fair amount of alcohol, drugs or peer pressure.

Once a crime is committed, the offender moves into a stage Clarke and Cornish define as the continuance model. At this level, the offender has experienced the success of committing a crime and enjoyed the benefits that come with it, including money, personal items, drugs, or merely the pure excitement of committing a crime. Successfully committing a crime once, or even several times, builds a sense of confidence in being able to engage in crime and get away with it. **The offender essentially confirms his skills at the particular crime and thinks that he is unlikely to be caught in the future. This fact alone explains why half of all crimes are committed by such a small percentage of criminals. They essentially begin to define themselves as criminals and believe that they are good at committing a specific type of crime. Success only leads to more criminal activity.**

Once engaged in crime the offender finds he is desperate for the easy money that crime provides, while shutting the door to most legitimate employment. The more crime a criminal engages in, the more contacts he develops in the criminal underground. He eventually finds someone who will quickly buy whatever he takes. Even if he only makes a few cents on the dollar, **the only cost to the offender is the risk**. Once he finds someone to sell stolen property to consistently, he grows confident that he can quickly pawn items for money. Such a profitable contact may only lead to other contacts in the criminal world. The offender soon finds he is more dependent on the income and the rush that comes with such crimes. Suddenly, trying to find legitimate work not only seems less profitable but it is also seen as much less exciting and glamorous. Once his circle of friends knows him as the guy who is a robber, or a burglar, or a shooter, he has developed a heck of a street cred. It is hard to give that up to flip burgers and soak fries for minimum wage.

Even if a criminal is arrested he learns the nature of the criminal justice system, and if the penalty does not outweigh the rewards, he is just as likely to continue in the behavior. An arrest will only put the offender in closer contact with other criminals who will support his type of behavior and reinforce his actions. Ultimately, the offender will begin to define himself as a particular kind of criminal, no different than most people define themselves by their career.

The final stage Clarke and Cornish identify is known as the desistance model. At this point the offender begins to reevaluate the crimes he is committing. A significantly bad event where he received little in payoff, or found himself confronted by a police K-9 who took 'a bite out of crime' might be a turning point for the offender. Add in a fair amount of wisdom that comes with age can dramatically change an offender's interest in crime. Blumstein and Cohen (1987) showed that as an individual grows into their early 20s the odds of committing crime drops by 50% and by age 28 drops by 85%.

In addition, the offender may undergo other life events such as marriage or a child that makes him reconsider the criminal lifestyle. At this point the criminal may begin to look for legitimate work that provides a consistent paycheck, or may simply search for an alternative form of crime viewed as less risky or more lucrative.

Clarke and Cornish present a case that criminal acts that the news would describe as random acts of crime are actually quite far from random. In fact, offenders make a number of calculated decisions before engaging in crime. The process may take only moments and become more efficient as the offender commits more crimes, but there are specific things offenders look for before, during, and after committing a crime to limit their risk and increase their reward.

This framework for understanding crime is really important if you want to decrease your likelihood of being a victim. Even today, much of criminology is still focused on what makes criminals different from the majority of law-abiding citizens. Criminologists try to determine if criminals are biologically different or do their social conditions lead to a life of crime. We will examine that briefly in the next section to better understand who are most likely to pose a threat, but knowing such information does little to prevent crime. Clarke and Cornish believed that by understanding that criminals do make multiple calculations of their risks, it becomes possible for each of us to take measures that makes targeting us appear too risky.

To see what things criminals look for when planning a crime, particularly violent crime, Wright and Decker (1997) studied 86 active armed robbers to gain a better understanding of their thought process in planning a robbery. The researchers found that the robbers consistently engaged in a number of rational decisions such as who to target, where, and how to approach the victim.

They found that the majority of robbers were poorly educated with few prospects beyond minimum wage jobs. Their addiction to drugs and alcohol made them unreliable for even the most menial jobs and their criminal backgrounds kept them out of most legitimate forms of work. This meant most robbers spent their existence in a state of financial crisis. They committed robbery to satisfy an immediate need for money that generally would be spent on drugs and alcohol. You find no Robin Hoods in crime. Robberies weren't committed for such noble causes as feeding children or providing needed medicine, it is for a continuation of a lifestyle of street culture focused on self-indulgence and nonstop partying. Essentially **those that are drawn to robbery and violent crimes live in the moment and seek only to satisfy their own needs.**

Although a robber could choose alternative crimes, robberies best suit their immediate needs. For most robbers, burglary simply poses too many risks. A robber realizes that entering a home meant that he runs too high a risk of being detected by the owner or a dog in an environment where the criminal does not have a tactical advantage over the victim in the same way as a street robbery. A homeowner knows the layout of the house. The robber doesn't. If a criminal planned to enter a house that was unoccupied he still ran too great a risk that the owner could come home at any moment. On the other hand, robbing a victim in the street allowed the offender to wait in a location that he can chose; a location that provides both shadows to conceal his presence and multiple avenues of escape before or after the event.

Most robbers consider dealing drugs as a means of getting what they want. However, most soon realize drug dealing requires too much risk with relatively minor payoff. Dealing put the offender at the risk of being attacked by another dealer, by a robber, or caught by the police. It was seen as hardly worth the effort. Unlike the other options available, robbery was seen as the safest and quickest way to cash.

With a primary driver of robbers being a need for cash to buy drugs, a majority of robbers see drug dealers as viable targets. Robbers rationalize that dealers carried the two things that they sought most, both drugs and money. Dealers do not deal in checks and credit cards; therefore they are likely to have a significant amount of cash on hand. They are also actively engaged in a felony, making them unlikely to report a crime. If they do, the police are likely to see it as a drug dealer being jumped and do little in follow-up investigation. This makes drug dealers a perfect target, aside from the high probability of the dealer having a gun.

This is important to understand when you hear crime reports on the news. **Many crime 'victims' are engaging in criminal behavior themselves.** That's what makes them such easy targets. They are putting themselves in contact with criminals and are less likely to report the crime to the police. If it is reported, the whole story rarely comes out. The 'victim' tells a half-truth to the police and then the police tell that to the media. The police don't share what they believe happen, as it might interfere with the investigation or even be slanderous. All of these things combined make it sound like a person, minding their own business, was jumped out of the blue. That certainly does happen, but it is rarely the case.

This also shows why such high percentages (44%) of victims are repeatedly victimized. Drug dealers understand that they will be robbed. It is just the nature of the job. However, to them the lure of big money from moving up from street hustler to a mid or high-level dealer is well worth the risks.

Female, armed robbers are even more likely to target those engaging in criminal or questionable behavior. It is rare for females to be armed robbers, but those who do tend to target middle-aged men looking for a prostitute. With the victim engaged in a criminal act, he is unlikely to report a crime that would expose his own indiscretion to the police and thus run the risk of his infidelity being revealed to his wife and family.

Robbers ultimately find a particular type of victim that they define as offering the greatest reward with the most limited risk. The only thing that varies is that each robber finds a type of person that they choose to specialize in robbing. For some, a White victim means less of a threat. To others, a Black victim is preferred with the assumption that a Black victim would carry more cash. Either way, **a person that openly displays their wealth with jewelry or cash is a far more attractive target.** A victim at an isolate ATM provides an ideal opportunity for a robber as the machine distracts the victim, has their back turned, and will soon have cash in hand. Similarly, robbers that target commercial establishments do so knowing that cash is readily available, something that cannot always be guaranteed in the street. Such robbers target stores with few employees and who do most of their business in cash. This decreases risk while increasing the payoff.

The increased use of credit cards today makes targeting individuals much less profitable for robbers. The robber pulls off a quick score with little problem from his victim, only to find a wallet filled with credit cards and no cash. Although a robber may have connections to sell the cards to, or can attempt to buy some items with the cards, each step only increases the chance that he will be caught. Because of this street robberies are on the decline. More robbers now target stores where they know cash is on hand. This means to be extra vigilant in locations that are likely to draw a robber. **Robbers look for businesses that deal primarily in cash and have few people in the location at any one time.**

In Wright and Decker's study most of the robbers chose handguns as their weapon of choice, even though knives are used 3 times as often in robberies as guns nationally. A handgun provides convincing proof of the offender's intentions, while allowing a robber to maintain distance from his victim. The bigger the gun the better its ability to get the immediate attention of the victim and the compliance the robber needs. Smaller caliber handguns may not pose enough threat to certain victims who may in turn challenge the robber. As odd as it sounds, this does happen. Less than a week ago, a robber attempted to rob a Domino's Pizza with a derringer. He leapt over the counter, pointed the diminutive pistol at the manager and demanded money. The manager shoed him out the door and chased him a block down the street before calling the police.

The majority of robbers do use knives, but it's usually as a last resort. To use a knife means acquiring a gun was too difficult and the need for a quick fix is too great. Knives put a robber at a distinct disadvantage in terms of the threat he poses and his distance from his victim. In Wright and Decker's study, the one male robber who relied on a knife for his robberies had the knife taken from him and was killed with it the very day they interviewed him. Females, on the other hand, are more likely to use knives. Females are more likely to lure a man into an isolated area with the expectation of sex. At this point the victim is naturally in much closer contact with the robber and usually in a highly vulnerable position when the knife is pulled.

Much of this represents the initial involvement stage where the robber prepares for a criminal act and who or what they would target. Once the offender finds the right victim in a location suitable enough to run the risk they will act. Each of the robbers interviewed developed a plan of attack that works for them. Some robbers prefer to sneak up and catch a victim by surprise; others would rather approach directly, letting the victim know what is happening. The robber then acts aggressively to scare the victim into following orders. If the victim fails to respond quickly enough, using physical force to get compliance is not out of the question.

Once robbers flee the scene, most look for routes that are difficult for automobile traffic. This limits the effectiveness of police attempting to quickly respond to the scene. In addition, most will commit crimes near their home, usually within a couple of blocks. This limits the timeframe that the police might have the opportunity to locate them. Very few robbers travel outside their neighborhood. This only puts robbers out of their own comfort zone and further from safety.

Although almost all robbers know what they are doing is wrong, few believe they have other alternatives. By their own assessment, their financial straits make robbery necessary. With such a view of themselves as being victims of society, continuing in robbery seems the only option for them. As part of the continuation model, they gain more and more success and recognize the relatively low chance of being caught. Each success confirms their beliefs about themselves and their decisions made toward appropriate targets, approaches, and locations.

Wright and Decker found that a number of the robbers that they interviewed would leave their criminal lifestyle if a good job were available. However, the reality of leaving crime is unlikely for most due to their criminal histories and addictions to drugs and alcohol that give them the personal characteristics most avoided by employers.

The benefit of Rational Choice Theory and Wright and Decker's study is that **we consistently see that criminals make multiple decisions about who or what to target. By understanding this we can use situational crime prevention to increase the criminal's perceived risks when sizing us up or targeting our property.** By making slight changes in our appearance or environment we can deter or eliminate the criminal's behavior (Schneider, 2010).

We will examine some of the characteristics of criminals next. It helps reveal the nature of persistent criminals so you can learn the specific steps you can take to make you and your property less inviting to criminals.

WHO ARE THE CRIMINALS?

Sept 30th 2014

At 1 pm thirteen shots echoed down the streets of a major intersection. Multiple witnesses watched as nine of the rounds found their mark, striking a repairman in the back of the head as he worked on a freestanding ATM. Police quickly responded, locking down the scene attempting to find the suspect. As police collected evidence and examined the scene their immediate thought was that this was a robbery gone terribly wrong.

Only a day later the suspect was in custody. The reason he gave for the shooting? He wasn't trying to take anything; he simply got into an argument with the repairman over not being able to access money from the ATM.

It simply defies common sense, but the offender believed he had been wronged and that justified him killing another human being. The murderer had largely rationalized his actions based on being inconvenienced. Within his mind such behavior was perfectly normal. Emile Durkheim (1893) explained such behavior as the result of a breakdown in social rules and behaviors. When society's norms no longer exist, new norms develop to fill the gap brought on by the criminal's social environment.

It many cases criminals find themselves drawn into crime, particularly violent crime, by a social strain, where their goals and expectations are limited by their own economic conditions. Rather than abide by the rules of society, they simply reject those norms and create their own (Merton, 1938). Such people may even develop contempt for the norms because everyone else in their immediate family and friends also reject the laws governing society. If they are raised in such an environment they essentially learn to become criminals (Bandura, 1977).

What that means is that **criminals are not regulated by society, but by their own peer group**. When people are not closely attached to parents or other positive networks they tend to become more delinquent. If they have no commitment to society, caring nothing for reputation or their own life, what is there to regulate their behavior? If they lack any involvement in work or school they have even fewer curbs to negative behavior and far more time to engage in such activities. If this leads a person to lose any real belief in the traits held as valuable to most of society there is nothing that morally constrains their behavior (Hirschi, 1969).

With such strong rejections of society, violence and disregard for others soon develop. Although this is true, the vast majority of people that are raised in such negative situations never become criminal. In fact, the kids that go on shooting sprees are from middle class families and reject society simply because they feel a sense of being an outcast.

The singular thing that ties all of these criminals together is a rejection of society. Whether the cause is extreme poverty or a complete disdain for their others, criminals consistently reject social convention. This is so prominent that 80% of those in prison have been diagnosed with Antisocial Personality Disorder. Of that group, 85% of them are in prison for acts of violence. People with Antisocial Personality Disorder make up only 1-4% of the general population of the country, but commit 90% of the crime.

Antisocial Personality Disorder is a catchall term that is frequently used synonymously with psychopath or sociopath. The common trait of these terms is a personality that lacks a compassion or affection for others. They are detached from others and don't feel basic human emotions such as guilt, remorse, or empathy. A sociopath can watch a horrific event play out and have no visible reaction. Because they can't feel love or build relationships with others their only use for others is to control them or win against them.

People with this personality disorder tend to show aggressive behavior at an early age. If it's allowed to continue without treatment it frequently grows into criminal behavior. If not, they become politicians. But then again, maybe I'm just repeating myself.

It is the people with this disorder that commit the majority of violent crime in America. The earlier the aggressive behavior starts, without an intervention, the worse it will get. Children that show an early onset of criminal behavior will tend to commit 40-700% more crime than those that enter into crime later in life. By the time a child reaches the age of 4 his or her behavior and self-control can predict how likely they will be to become involved in crime later in life with 85% accuracy.

The negative behaviors of asocial children are recognized frequently by peers and teachers, but are often dismissed by the parents. The kids that have psychopathic and criminal behaviors frequently display these traits:

Cruelty
Morbid fascination with violence and death
Threats or talk of killing others
Considered 'weird' or dangerous by peers
Uncontrollable temper
Narcissistic
Bedwetting

These are essentially narcissistic children that see others as pawns, rather than having empathy towards others. When you think of the teens involved in recent mass killings, the kids involved display a consistent pattern of antisocial behavior that is obvious from early in life. They only feed this antisocial behavior by engrossing themselves in first person shooter games that help lead to their final lashing out at society by acting out the video games in real life. It is their total lack of empathy with others that is so often seen in court when the elements of their crime are spelled out in detail. Although they know these things are wrong from society's perspective, they have no sense of it being morally reprehensible and remain emotionless in court.

Youth with asocial behavior will likely face arrest, become deceitful, show reckless disregard for their safety and others, will be unable to hold down a job, contract STDs, and have a 6 to 7 times higher mortality rate than other kids. These behaviors are obvious by the time they reach 4 years old and their life of crime tends to start as early as 10.

From a biological level, the genetic make-up of these kids has a significantly higher correlation to their criminal behavior than parental behavior. The whole debate of what has more impact on a child's development, nature over nurture, seems to be leaning heavily towards nature at this point. Studies of adopted children shows that they consistently display behavior closer to their biological parents than to their adopted parents.

The kids that show these early behavioral traits are called Life Course Persistent offenders (Moffitt, 1993). Their deviant behaviors simply never go away. They will always display disorderly or criminal behavior throughout their life unless they are spotted and treated at an early age. If they start receiving treatment only after they reach their teen years, or while in prison, it is unlikely that anything can be done to change their criminal actions.

This small group makes up less than 4% of the population but accounts for most of the crime. However, almost all juveniles do go through a period where they begin to engage in dangerous and sometimes criminal behavior. Normal brain development helps explain why juvenile delinquency occurs. Brain scans show that adolescent brains are not fully functioning, confirming everything you always thought about kids; they simply are not in their right minds. What brain scans show is that adolescents do not have a fully developed frontal cortex. This causes them to engage in far more risky behavior, as they can't fully understand environmental input. When this is combined with a decrease in wanting to please their parents as much as they want to appeal to their peers you can understand why most teens become involved in some form of delinquent behavior. However, while these Adolescent–Limited offenders might engage in crime, they will grow out of their delinquent behavior by their early twenties.

The thing that sets Life Course Persistent offenders apart from Adolescent-Limited offenders is that their frontal cortex never fully develops. The neurological connects that would allow them to make good decisions just don't occur. They operate under self-interest, becoming easily bored, lacking empathy, and blaming others for their problems. Their ability to be responsible, logical, or self-controlled is grossly underdeveloped. They find it difficult to be patient, which makes anything they want into something they need and need right now. Without a fully developed frontal lobe criminal behavior continues well into adulthood and tends to cause greater risks of violent behavior because they react emotionally to every event. These career criminal offenders will show a lot of continuity in criminal behavior from early in life. Most will not specialize in one type of crime. They will merely look for whatever opportunity comes their way. They may comprise a small segment of the population, but they will cause nearly half of all crime. Although this group is called Life Course Persistent, 85% of these career criminals will decrease their criminal behavior by age 29. At that age they've gained enough social bonds, usually a wife and kids that act as outside influences and restraints to their criminal behavior.

In addition to the asocial behavior, the majority of criminals are male. Men commit 89% of all murders, 80% of violent crime, and 63% of property crime. This is consistent throughout the criminal justice system. Women engage in significantly fewer crimes than men. They also enter into the system in a decidedly different way. While men self-identify themselves by their criminal behavior, women are far less likely to do so, with most being drawn into crime by either a male companion or by his abuse. Women that commit crime are far more likely to be engaged in prostitution or embezzlement than any other crime. Unlike men, who frequently are driven to satisfy immediate needs, women are more likely seeking financial gain in order to support their children. They may be dealing with their own victimization or looking for a means of coping with bad relationships through drugs or alcohol that often lead them further into a life of deviancy. They are far less likely to engage in violent behavior unless engaging in it with a male partner.

Criminal Summary

From this, you can draw a reasonable, but not all-inclusive, idea of who is most likely to target you for crime. Generally offenders are males that range in age from 15-28 years old. They will not have an adult offering supervision and may be operating along with other teens, or young adults, spurring their behavior. They will most likely have a history that includes:

Cruelty
Morbid fascination with violence and death
Threats or talk of killing others
Considered 'weird' or dangerous by peers
Uncontrollable temper
Narcissistic

Fortunately, these people only make up a very small percentage of the population. They are a small group that is biologically driven to bad behavior. Asocial personalities react like a 3-year-old seeing candy in a checkout lane. Whatever they want they think they need and they think they need it right now. They will do whatever is necessary to get what they want if they see no immediate risk. Their behavior tends to be violent and is combined with a lack of compassion. They simply do not have the ability to empathize with their victims.

Because they comprise such a small segment of society, your odds of being violently victimized are very low if you yourself are not engaging in questionable behavior. However, it also means that if you are confronted, you should understand how dangerous this particular segment of society is and be willing to react accordingly.

RACE AND CRIME

With two legal decisions in Ferguson, Missouri and New York City that exonerated police officers in the deaths of two Black men the issue of race and the criminal justice system has come under an electron microscope of public opinion. The argument is that the police and the whole criminal justice system are both set up unfairly against Blacks.

What the people pushing the racial bias agenda cite is the high percentage of Black men in prison in relation to the overall population. They argue that Blacks only represent 13% of the population but make up 56% of the prison population. With that statistic alone you could argue a biased system all day long. Many people are more than eager to do just that, though often more for there own self-interest than to solve the problem they are claiming. What this statistic does is look simply at the world as a Black and White issue, viewing people only as members of a group rather than as individuals. However, if individual factors are considered, suddenly things aren't so Black and White after all.

The first factor to look at is the nature of the neighborhood in which a crime occurs. More than forty years ago, Egon Bittner (1970) began to examine the neighborhoods where police typically work. Bittner found that police are deployed in areas of town where more crime is likely to occur. Minorities make up the vast portion of these neighborhoods that are usually plagued with poverty. Bittner argued that given those circumstance, even an impartial officer would be justified in being suspicious of a young, Black male whose actions drew the officer's attention, more than the actions of an older, White person in a higher income area. Bittner realized that an unbiased officer would be more likely to stop a Black youth due to the nature of the high crime and low income area of town where the officer works, rather than the subject's race.

Bittner argued that certain areas of society contribute disproportionately to the level of crime. The police are expected to control crime and keep the peace. If law enforcement failed to be suspicious of activity in an economically disadvantaged area simply because of the racial make-up of the community they would be equally condemned for not doing their job. This would lead to the police being viewed as illegitimate and unresponsive to the needs of the neighborhood (Kirk & Matsuda, 2011).

This reveals that when examining the idea of racial discrimination in the criminal justice system it becomes necessary to consider neighborhood context. More crime is likely to occur in economically depressed areas. Unfortunately, a greater number of minorities live in these poor neighborhoods. These areas also tend to be in large urban communities, the very locations where more law enforcement officers work. Douglas Smith (1986) studied sixty neighborhoods and found that the lower the socioeconomic status of a neighborhood, the greater the chance of arrest or use of force. Smith found that it was the nature of the neighborhood that led to the actions, independent of the type of offense, or the race of the suspect.

Terrill and Mastrofski, (2002) also confirmed that race has statistically no influence over police behaviors when it comes to arrest, or the use of force, once the nature of the neighborhood is considered. They found that police are more likely to use force in high crime areas and concentrated disadvantage, without regard to race. These areas are viewed by police as dangerous places, which leads the police to respond with higher levels of force (Herbert, 1998).

This finding was also confirmed by a study conducted by researchers Werthman and Piliavin (1967). Their study of both Oakland and San Francisco, CA found that officers define geographic areas as suspicious or dangerous places. From the police officer's experience he knows these areas are more likely in poorer sections of town. It is the socioeconomic character of the neighborhood and not a suspect's personal characteristics that draw police attention. It is not that officers are biased along racial lines, rather the neighborhoods that officers patrol tend to be lower income and have a higher concentration of minorities. It is the economic nature of the community that leads to the inequality seen between Whites and other races within the criminal justice system.

This neighborhood context also applies to traffic stops. A driver's chances of being pulled over by police will be influenced by the location of the stop, the time of day, erratic driving, and vehicle type or condition, completely independent of the driver's race (Engel, et at, 2005). From personal experience, many times traffic stops are made where it is either too dark, or the tint on the windows makes it impossible, to know the race of the occupants, or even the number of people in the car. The reason for the stop considers the totality of the circumstances and is dependent on the driver's actions, not on the driver's race. Once stopped, the driver's verbal and nonverbal behaviors that appear suspicious, deceptive, or aggressive will likely lead to a more thorough investigation than a polite individual with nothing to hide (Engel, et at, 2005; Engel, Tillyer & Cherkauskas, 2007).

The socioeconomic nature of the neighborhood is consistent with the "broken windows" theory of Wilson and Kelling (1982). They stated that areas appearing disorderly and out-of-control cultivate a climate for violent crime. In a neighborhood where a minor issue such as a broken window is not fixed, than other, more severe crimes are likely to occur. When economically depressed neighborhoods are considered, racial biases are statistically insignificant across multiple studies. This applies to traffic stops, arrests, and use of force.

Beyond the neighborhood context, those that argue a racial bias among the police don't recognize how police end up investigating an offense. Much of what the police do is reactive and not proactive policing. That means that police are responding to reports of crime and not acting on their own self-initiated activity (Goldstein, 1979). Many times the criminal justice system begins with a victim's decision to contact the police. In addition, victims only report an estimated half of all crime (USDJ, 2010). These victims control law enforcement's arrest practices in two ways. By not contacting the police, citizens are already limiting the criminal justice system from acting on a suspect. If the police are called, they are again limited in making an arrest based on the victim's preferences. Unless law requires an arrest, the victim can request that the police simply resolve the situation without taking anyone into custody (Gottfredson & Gottfredson, 1988). Although police do have a great amount of discretion, most arrests are based on the wants of the victim. This again shows that the police are not discriminating on race, but merely carrying out the request of a victim when using the law.

According the FBI's Uniform Crime Report from 2011, 70% of people arrested are White and slightly less than 30% are Black. From this, we can see that a ratio far closer to the actual population enters the criminal justice system. If that's the case, what accounts for the disparity seen in the prison population? The primary reasons people go to prison are based on three factors: The person's past criminal history, the violence of the criminal act committed, and the defendant's relationship to the victim. These are the elements that both judges and juries look at in determining sentencing simply because the first and third determine the likelihood that the defendant will repeat the crime while the severity of the crime determines penalty. When these factors are considered, suddenly race is no longer a factor. The color of the defendant disappears and what is considered is what that INDIVIDUAL did to go to prison.

Some crimes are simply not important enough to report to the police. They may involve matters that the victim would rather settle privately. In some cases, victims realize that there is little chance that someone would be arrested, or that it is unlikely that missing items would ever be recovered. In those instances, crimes simply aren't reported.

In those cases where crimes are reported, Lawrence M. Friedman and Robert V. Percival (1981) developed the "wedding cake" model to explain the criminal justice process. This model explains how cases are not treated equally by the criminal justice system. At the top of the cake are the high profile cases such as O.J. Simpson or George Zimmerman that reach national attention.

The second tier of the cake is serious felonies such as murder, rape, or robbery. At this level the victim is likely to have been injured by the accused or had a weapon used against them. These are high profile cases and put pressure on prosecutors to seek a longer sentence for the accused.

 The third tier is lesser felonies such as thefts or breaking and entering cases where no weapon was used. The fourth layer consists of misdemeanors, or minor citation arrests. These arrests make up more than three-quarters of all arrests made by police and are handled informally by the court system.

The criminal justice system is not rigged against Blacks. Justice is blind to all but a criminal's history, the violent nature of his act, and his relationship to the victim. To understand this we simply have to look at some facts that include not only the person's race, but also the crime committed. FBI arrest records from 2012 indicate that 44,000 Blacks were arrested for robbery, while only 34,000 Whites were arrested for the same crime. Blacks were arrested for 4200 murders while Whites were arrested for 4100 murders. This is an almost identical number, despite Whites comprising a significantly greater amount of the population. What this makes clear is that although Blacks represent a small fraction of the population, they commit a significantly greater amount of violent crime.

This is not a bash against a race, but to clarify the facts and to point out something even more disturbing. Although Blacks are more likely to engage in violent behavior, they are also more likely to be the victims of that same violent crime. Despite only making up 13% of the population, Blacks are the victims of nearly half of all murders. Rather than Black murders being somehow racially motivated, Black's commit 93% of the murders of other Blacks. In an almost identical statistic 86% of White's murdered are committed by another White. This is because someone that knows the victim commits most homicides. The real crime of the race debate is that Black advocates will never address this issue. If Black lives truly matter, then they matter no matter who pulls the trigger.

When you look at the facts, rather than the hype, it becomes clear that the reasons for the amount of Blacks in prison is not related to a bias in the system, but rather a culture that promotes violence. As we discussed in the section entitled 'Who are the Criminals', we find that those most likely to commit crime are generally males that range in age from 15-28 years old. They will not have an adult offering supervision and may be operating along with other teens, or young adults, that either push or pull them into criminal behavior. They are more likely to exist in an environment that rejects social norms and learn to become criminals. It is this very segment of young, Black men that are being fed a constant diet of rap music and movies that degrade women, glamorizes drug use, and promotes a gang lifestyle. The role models that they are presented with are often former pimps, drug dealers, and gang members rather than doctors, businessmen, or engineers.

When the party culture being pushed by the media is combined with the stunning fact that 70% of all Blacks are born to single parent homes compared to only 28% of White children the real problem becomes apparent. The single best predictor of poverty in America is a family where a single female is the head of the household. While White children may grow up in a similar household and in poverty, they are likely to be surrounded by others of differing economic means. They have the benefit of seeing other role models that engage in some work that provides a better lifestyle. On the other hand, poor Black children are more likely to grow up in urban environments of concentrated poverty where all the families are poor and very few fathers are present. Most of the adults they know exist on welfare or minimum wage jobs. This area is called a Zone of Transition (Park & Burgess, 1925) where those with the economic means to leave will do so as soon as they have the financial ability to leave. That makes those with no ability to leave trapped in a landscape of poverty with no positive role models or influences. Frequently, the only sign of success within such a culture are those that sell drugs.

With these poor children growing up with only their mother for supervision they often lack a positive male role model and any consistent parental oversight. The mother is all too often missing due to work or her own party lifestyle. Those kids that are capable of achieving academically and could escape their circumstances are degraded by their peers and often have to mimic a tough, street attitude to survive their environment. Without any real guidance or strong family structure these kids find a sense of belonging and perceived protection among a group by joining gangs. But rather than finding a protection from violence, they now become all the more likely to be the targets of other gangs. It is this drug and gang related violence that explains the higher murder rate seen among Blacks and also to the higher percentage of Blacks seen in the prison population.

Those that promote a race bias are correct that there is a systemic problem, but it is not a problem within the criminal justice system. It is a far deeper problem of a welfare system that holds people in poverty and dependent on government. Welfare in its current form is not designed as a means of escaping one's circumstances, but is designed to keep those on welfare perpetually poor. It intentionally or unintentionally promotes single parent homes by giving additional benefits to single mothers rather than to families that stay together. By doing so it has caused Black families to triple in the number of single parent households compared to what were seen in the early 1960s.

If looked at through Black and White glasses, with no other factors, the courts appear biased. But once you see the other underlying issues such as violence and criminal history things fall more into perspective. It could be argued that the police are overly racist in the way they interact between Whites and Blacks. However, if you look at the FBI's Uniform Crime Reports it shows that there are an average of 14,172,384 arrests made by law enforcement each year. Of that number 70% of the arrest are of Whites and only 600 to 700 led to the death of the suspect. Less than 400 of those deaths are related directly to the actions of law enforcement. There doesn't appear to be a system wide bias within the criminal justice system that is leaving young Black men dead throughout this country. In fact, data collected by the Bureau of Justice Statistics (1996) shows that less than .3% of arrests involve any physical force at all. Violence to gain compliance is very rare even in law enforcement. When it does happen, it can often be again tied to the suspect's violent actions and an extensive criminal history.

When you look at your odds of being a crime victim these facts should be considered. **Statistics on violent crimes may appear to be incredibly high in your city, but often this crime is highly localized to certain places and individuals that are engaging primarily in a drug or gang lifestyle. The criminals will be repeat offenders and the victims will be repeat victims. They are also likely to exchange roles. The lifestyle they lead is promoted by the media and is fueled by a breakdown in both families and the neighborhood support system that would prevent such behavior.** In such neighborhoods there is no longer a sense of watching out for each other, but of watching out simply for themselves.

If there were real interest in solving the problem of bias seen in crime it would not look at the police or the courts. It would first need to address a welfare system that promotes the destruction of the family. Instead of paying more benefits to single parent homes it would reward families for staying together to the benefit of the children. It would also need to be reformed to not end benefits as soon as work is found. It would offer incentives to move off of welfare, but continue to provide support as people pull themselves out of poverty. Until such actions are taken, the high rate of crime seen among inner city youth will continue.

Advocates of bias in policing are not completely without merit. The current social structure of concentrated poverty and gang violence causes policing to be handled differently within poor, Black neighborhoods. Because violent crime is far more common in these communities and there are more people in these areas you are more likely to see more police and they are more likely to make arrests. Because crime rates are so high, frequently mayors and city councils want the police to take a zero tolerance approach to crime. The idea is to enforce minor crimes to prevent major crimes from occurring. This developed out of the Broken Windows Theory (Wilson & Kelling, 1982) that states once one window is broken in a neighborhood and not fixed it will promote other windows to be broken. In essence, if small things are not corrected it will lead to more and greater problems in a neighborhood. To prevent drug sales and shootings, some cities expect the police to enforce jaywalking and littering at a far greater rate in these neighborhoods than they would in middleclass neighborhoods. This approach has been effective at times, but it does nothing to build relationships between the police and the communities they serve. It does nothing to try to solve the underlying social issues. If done poorly and without community support, it only builds resentment among the population and less likelihood for anyone to call the police, thus creating a downward spiral of even more crime.

Rather than crying racism while ransacking stores and stealing TVs and liquor, perhaps there should be a rational approach to trying to improve social conditions among the urban poor. Much could be accomplished if both sides worked towards welfare reform and towards building relationships between the police and the community.

A final thought, the Bureau of Justice Statistics shows that 82% of felony defendants in the largest counties are male. Men make up 99% of all rape suspects, commit 96% of all weapon related offenses, commit 90% of all robberies, and 93% of all murders (Cohen & Reaves, 2006). Is that because the criminal justice system is biased against men? No, the simple fact is that men cause more of these criminal offenses. This is a similar issue to consider when examining race in the criminal justice system.

The reason that minorities are disproportionately represented in the criminal justice system is not based on racial bias, but begins because minorities are more likely to live in urban neighborhoods that are economically depressed and high in crime. Because these neighborhoods suffer high amounts of crime, police are more likely to be called to respond to criminal behavior. For a witness or victim to call the police it requires that the crime to be serious enough to involve the criminal justice system, because most minor crimes will simply go unreported. When police respond to a crime they are more likely to find the suspect is a young, male, minority. Like the high number of men seen in the criminal justice system, it is not that the system is biased, but that young, Black men simply commit more serious crimes and they commit these crimes more often. The criminal justice system treats these violent crimes very seriously. Once arrested, the suspect's prior record will determine if the court system believes the risk of allowing the defendant to go free outweighs the risk to the community.

When all these items are considered, the decisions that lead a person through the criminal justice system are made on legally relevant factors and do not discriminate based on the offender's race.

Much of what we hear in the media about race and crime has no basis in reality. That's why it's important to address the issue here. Primarily, the purpose of this chapter is to get beyond the shouts and slogans and look at the facts that surround violent crime. **The reality is that if you are a poor Black in an urban environment you will face a far higher likelihood of being a victim of violent crime, particularly if you become involved in a gang or party lifestyle. Whites are less likely to be victims of violent crime, but like Blacks are more likely to be attacked by someone of their own race. These are not racial issues, but purely about opportunity. Criminals may target a particular race, but they generally are looking for the easiest opportunity.**

In the next chapter, we will look further into policing and examine if you truly want to base your personal safety on your ability to call the police. Are the police your best means of security, or is your personal safety your responsibility?

POLICING

The police do not prevent crime. This is one of the best-kept secrets of modern life. The police know it, public officials know it, but the public does not know it - Bayley, 1994.

Having looked at who criminals are and looking at the reality of race in crime, we should look closer at the 'thin blue line' that is supposed to keep criminals in check. Although we have touched briefly on policing, it's a topic that we should explore further primarily because of the statement made by Bayley. It reveals an underlying truth in law enforcement that most people simply don't consider. Police departments, because of the founder's concerns over rights and liberties, are largely responsive to crimes rather than proactive in preventing crimes. Unlike the NSA and other questionable federal agencies that seem to be pushing the limits of what they can legally do, the police primarily respond for calls from the public, rather than preventing crime from occurring.

Policing, as we know it today largely developed in England under Sir Robert Peel to act as an extension of the public. The police were supposed to be members of the community that maintained order by enforcing the laws that were held in common agreement by the population. This concept was soon adopted in the United States. Unfortunately, being under the hand of politicians, many departments soon became nothing more than tools of intimidation by corrupt political machines to defeat opponents and remain in power.

It wasn't until the early 20th Century that police administrators sought to break from the corruption of political machines. The reform minded executives set about creating professional law enforcement agencies. O.W. Wilson (1963) developed the idea of officers patrolling in marked vehicles on random preventive patrol, reasoning that if police were constantly patrolling the public and criminals would feel that the police were omnipresent. As these officers patrolled they were expected to respond rapidly to citizen complaints or roll up on criminals and catch them in the act. If the police did this they were seen as professional law enforcement and would be seen as legitimate by the public (Kelling & Morre, 1988).

This understanding of how policing should be conducted became institutionalized over time. For a police agency to be seen as legitimate it had to conduct random vehicle patrol, respond rapidly to calls for service, utilize cutting edge technology for investigation, and organize themselves as a paramilitary unit to be seen as professional by citizens and other police organizations (Crank & Langworthy, 1992). However, much of this was done with little focus on if it was effective at preventing crime. In reality, these activities did not serve the purpose of efficiency or performance, but merely the myth of how a police agency should act (Meyer and Rowan, 1977).

What this means is that many police and sheriff departments remain locked into an institutional theory of how they should act, rather than seeking to solve criminal problems, or correct harms before they happen. Police still rely primarily on the public to identify something questionable occurring and asking officers to investigate. This places law enforcement in the position of responding to a call for service and attempting to solve that single issue, rather than seeing a pattern of problems developing and attempting to prevent a crime from occurring in the first place. As mentioned in the previous chapter, this is one of the factors so often missed, or deliberately obscured, by those claiming racial bias in policing. The primary reason police show up at a location is due to a call from a citizen. The reason so many police respond and patrol primarily Black neighborhoods, is because of a higher number of calls by a witness or a victim, not because the police are targeting a specific race.

However, this traditional method of policing may not be the best way to decrease crime. The current model is to have the police respond to crime, report on it, investigating it, and use the criminal law to arrest, or deter offenders. This is the same whether the behavior is a noise complaint or a homicide. All too often situations that involve solving problems that might prevent crimes from happening are seen as being outside the scope of professional law enforcement and rather the responsibility of social agencies (Kelling & Morre, 1988). However, as Malcolm Sparrow (2008) explained it is only when specific harms are identified that interventions can be developed to prevent crimes.

So what we see today in policing is that law enforcement agencies don't develop around solving criminal problems. Instead they organize around well-established functions and processes that other organizations use. After all, how do you prove how effective you are at preventing a crime that never happens? It is far easier to show that officers have ten traffic tickets, ten parkers, and ten misdemeanor arrests each month. Such measurable results are an easy way for police agencies to show productivity to the public, even if it isn't effective at doing the task they're expected to perform. That's the major problem of many governmental bureaucracies. At the end of the day, they don't produce anything of value. There's no truck, home, or television built. This means the police cannot really measure their inputs or outputs of goods, so they simply rely on mimicking other forms of organizations where something is produced so that they appear to be professional (DiMaggio & Powell, 1983).

The sad truth is that most law enforcement agencies operate this way. Crime prevention is not the objective. Police administrators are all too often locked into the idea that an officer's ability in the street is gauged by nonsense numbers such as the number of traffic tickets and parking violations written. This is a focus on work product that doesn't lead to an overall decrease in crime, only an enforcement of laws.

So, when you think that it is the job of the police to prevent and protect you from crime, you can see that most policing organizations all too often fall short of that objective. The whole agency gets caught up in the idea that this is the way we've always dealt with crime. It's only recently that academics and the police have come together to try to limit crime through a scientific approach. As we covered earlier, only a small number of locations lead to half or more of all crime. To be effective, both Koper (1995) and Sherman (1990) found that police should move from one high crime location to another high crime location, rather than patrolling in a neighborhood pattern. The police can target a sizable amount of citywide crime simply by focusing on a small number of high crime locations (Weisburd & Telep, 2010). Although this targeted approach towards crime has been shown to work, random patrols of neighborhoods in areas of little crime still remains the norm.

Even fewer agencies spend time trying to figure out what makes a location a high crime area. Such a novel approach might reduce or eliminate crime in an area altogether. If the police simply asked, "is there something about this location that makes it an opportunity for crime?" Then the police or another agency might be able to fix that problem. Even better, if the police asked, "who is the owner of the location and what can he do that he isn't to prevent crime?" If an owner or agency can eliminate something that makes a location low risk for offenders, such as razing a vacant building or removing graffiti and trash, crime in the area will decrease, even if it displaces somewhere nearby. Even if the crime moves, the new location is unlikely to be as conducive to crime; otherwise the offender would have chosen that location to begin with. Such a problem solving approach to high crime locations has shown to decrease violent crime by 33% even 90 days after the police stop addressing the issue (Taylor, Koper, & Woods, 2011).

Despite the image that Hollywood gives of the police as constantly chasing criminals or diligently investigating a crime, you can see that the truth behind law enforcement is far more complex. For the most part agencies operate from a basic idea of enforcing traffic violations and minor crimes and responding to calls for service, oftentimes acting as little more than social workers or secretaries with guns. As much as the public and cops themselves want to view the role of police as crime fighters, the majority of calls are dealing with ongoing family issues that have been brewing for years. The police respond to these problems and put a Band-Aid on the issue until it blows up again. Crimes themselves are viewed in much the same way. Each crime is viewed as an individual case to be investigated. If the cops are lucky they get a conviction in the case and it is classified as 'solved.' However, that doesn't stop the underlying reason why the crime is occurring and how it can be stopped. **Most police agencies are not looking to prevent crime, merely the investigation and prosecution of it.**

If you don't want to have to deal with officers responding to investigate a crime against you and possibly identify a suspect, then the responsibility of crime prevention rests on you.

PLACE

When a place is not clear for legitimate use, criminals will find illegitimate uses for it. - John Eck

What reasonable steps can you take to prevent crime? The first step is to understand one of the most significant developments in crime science in the past two decades called the Crime Analyst Triangle. This idea builds on Routine Activities Theory that we covered earlier. Very simply, in order for any crime to occur there are three things that have to come together: an offender, victim, and a location. The location itself doesn't have to be physical; it can be the World Wide Web. But the concept is that by removing any one of these items from the equation can prevent a crime from happening.

Image courtesy of the Center for Problem-Oriented Policing

However, law enforcement agencies typically only deal with one of these three issues. Police target offenders and hope to arrest them. The problem is, you are almost always dependent on the offender committing the crime before you can act. **To prevent crime you need to examine what can be done to change the behavior of the victim, or what can be done to make a location less conducive to crime.** It is far more effective to protect a possible victim, or harden a location, than to predict who will commit a crime and when.

If a willing offender finds a suitable target in an area with little oversight the chances of a crime occurring increase dramatically. To prevent crime you have to determine what makes certain places far more likely to draw crime.

One of the most common causes is how convenient the location is for both parties to meet. As an example, highway off ramps in urban areas tends to draw a significant amount of crime. In most major cities, a person needing a fix of heroin, crack, or marijuana can quickly exit the freeway, turn onto a major artery and receive drive-up service that would rival Wendy's and Burger King. The same driver could just as quickly get back onto the freeway and slip out of the area before anyone could even think to call the cops.

Brantingham and Brantingham (1999) confirmed the idea that the nature of certain locations makes them conductive to crime by placing offenders and targets in locations convenient for crime. These areas are where criminals are likely to frequent in their daily life and victims are likely to pass through during the course of their day. Their review of the literature showed that burglary, robbery, and even serial murder are shaped directly by highway exits and road networks.

In addition, Brantingham and Brantingham's (1995) Crime Pattern Theory identified four different types of locations and their effect on crime. These areas they defined as crime generators, crime attractors, crime-neutral, and fear generators.

Crime generators bring a large number of people to a single location, making the area a target rich environment. A park-and-ride or parking garages represent just such locations. In either spot, an offender can safely gauge the time a victim might be away from their vehicle with little chance of being detected. After all, everyone else who parked there is on a similar time schedule. Although the offender may not have been there to commit a crime, the situation makes the odds of being caught so low that breaking into a car or two might be worth the risk.

Crime attractors, on the other hand, are areas that are known locations where questionable behavior is expected to occur. Entertainment districts with a cluster of bars, open-air drug markets, or street segments known for prostitution are just such locations. These are spots that have a built in history of criminal activity and tend to draw people that want to engage in criminal behavior. A shopping mall for a shoplifter offers ample opportunity and would naturally attract a specific type of crime.

Crime attractors are important because they are also the type of area that would be a prime location for a terrorist attack. Here a small number of people could cause a significant amount of physical harm. Terrorists think in terms of large numbers of people, little defense, and the possibility of disabling infrastructure at the same time. Four or five terrorist cells with only a handful of radicals could strike elementary schools throughout the country and simply devastate our ability to trust our government to protect our children or us. An attack at a subway, train, or bus complex could harm hundreds or thousands and shut down mass transit for months or years. Both attacks wouldn't require guns, but simple homemade bombs.

Crime neutral locations do not bring offenders and victims together in any specific manner. An offender neither goes to the locations to commit a crime, nor are they likely to find a target rich environment if they happen to be there.

The remaining location is referred to as a fear generator. These locations cause an individual to feel at risk and have little control over the area. This can be a neighborhood marked with graffiti and trash or a dark alley that makes a person feel uncertain of what might be lurking in the shadows. These areas give the sense of 'no one cares', consistent with what Wilson and Kelling (1982) defined as Broken Window's. As we covered earlier these areas give criminals the sense that if the small stuff is not fixed or reported then we can get away with almost anything. The criminals realize that there is less guardianship over these areas to prevent them from committing crime. Victims in these areas also sense that they could be targeted at any moment.

As you can see, locations are important because they can directly affect the amount and nature of crime that occurs. **Areas rich in potential targets, a history of questionable behavior, or a location** that shows a breakdown of social control will naturally attract offenders looking for an opportunity.

This understanding can help you to be defensive in locations that are likely to increase your risks. It is not always possible to avoid such locations. As you can see, just the process of going about your day to day responsibilities may put you into one or more of these locations at various points in your day.

As an example of a place you might pass through in your daily life lets look at the New York Port Authority. It serves passengers from 6,822 buses a day as they travel in and out of the city for legitimate business. However, the location also became the hangout for a wide assortment of homeless, drug addicts, prostitutes, and con men looking to prey on people as they went about their daily routine. To address these issues the bus terminal underwent changes in the early 1990s to use environmental design to make the location less of a crime attractor and generator. By redesigning the way the 1.5 million square feet of space was used these problems were significantly decreased and a sense of safety returned to the legitimate users of the terminal.

Areas under stairways that allowed for vagrants to camp out were enclosed and became closets. Recessed doorways that allowed for covert behavior were pushed out to be flush with the surrounding walls to prevent such nooks from hiding illicit activity. A rarely used entrance was converted into a coffee shop that provided natural surveillance. Improved lighting was added throughout the building and the floors were treated with high gloss sealer that provided additional brightness to the area. Large columns that developed into resting areas were either made smaller to increase the flow of foot traffic, or retail stores were pushed out to encompass the columns to redirect traffic. Benches that acted as beds for the homeless were replaced by fold down chairs. Bathrooms that were a haven for disorder were significantly changed, with ceiling panels secured so that the area above the bathrooms could no longer be accessed. Individual sinks replaced the one long sink that often served as a bath for the homeless. Businesses were placed near the bathrooms for additional surveillance and gates were added to cut the bathrooms in half after the morning and evening rush hour (Felson, et al, 1996).

Most of the steps did not come at significant expense, but were simply means of reexamining the space and the way it was being used. What this shows is that by **making simple changes to a location you can dramatically decrease the ease of committing crime or if criminals will be drawn to an area**. However, not every location has taken the time to make the changes necessary to prevent opportunities for crimes. That's why it becomes important to be aware of things in your immediate environment that might be conducive to crime. When you notice large columns, alcoves under stairways, or doorways that can conceal someone you should be alert that someone might be using those areas to wait for an unsuspecting victim. Simply giving yourself distance from such elements in your immediate environment gives you additional time to react and decrease opportunities for a criminal to attack. **Criminals frequently need an element of surprise. By remaining aware of such things in your environment you can take actions that removes the element of surprise from offenders and takes away their opportunity.**

Parking lots and garages are other large areas that are frequently used for crime. They are locations that have a large number of potential victims, but tend to have a low amount of foot traffic at any one time. That means there might be hundreds or thousands of potential victims, but only one in a certain location at a time. This increases the likelihood of violent criminal behavior. By being aware of these areas you can decrease your chance at being a victim. By redesigning these spaces opportunities for crime can be eliminated.

The single most important step in preventing crime in such areas is increased lighting. Proper lighting has been documented to lower crime in parking facilities consistently (Smith, 1996). Simply using a clear stain on a concrete floor to increase brightness of a garage by reflecting the existing light can also be effective.

The second most important measure to preventing crime is allowing for natural surveillance. In parking garages this involves minimizing the slope of the ramps and seeking openness within the structure, such as opening stairways so that they are visible to the outside, preventing criminals from remaining hidden. In addition, posting signs to help direct legitimate users out of the facility quickly or back to their car easily helps people avoid victimization.

Parking garages pose a lot of potential danger. They are by their nature large with multiple levels and are easily accessible by everyone, allowing offenders to fit in with legitimate users. The traffic patterns are irregular, leading to victim isolation while other parked cars provide cover. If you think of yourself in a parking garage, there is generally a sense of foreboding. However, if you are on a floor that is open to the outside there tends to be a decrease in the anxiety you feel when compared to a location that is underground. The first provides both more natural light and the sense that someone might see or hear an attack occurring inside the facility.

In a similar fashion, a garage that has a staircase that is open to the outside seems much less confining and dangerous than an enclosed stairwell that has graffiti on the walls and little opportunity to see who or what might lay in wait around the next corner.

You can't control the design of the buildings that you enter in your daily activities. It's simply a fact of life. However, **it's important that you understand that a place that makes you feel uncomfortable because it's confined and dark has an opposite effect on a criminal.** Knowing that criminals think rationally you can assume that they will take advantage of such locations to hide their crime. In such a case, you need to be particularly aware of the people and sounds around you. In these locations you should attempt to park nearest to the ground level and the closer to an exit the better. Each flight of stairs and each step you can avoid will decrease your opportunity to be victimized.

Like parking complexes, convenience stores can become crime attractors because of the cash nature of the business. They make purchases of small items easy for customers, but make robbing them equally easy to criminals. It's here where the design of the business comes into play and dramatically alters the opportunity for crime to occur.

A convenience store with large windows that allow you to see clearly into the interior gives you a sense of comfort knowing that you can see if anything is wrong inside. From the lot you can see down each aisle and can see almost every area of the business. A clerk working inside at a register facing the door is able to watch the lot. The customers provide natural security to the business, and the clerk provides security to both the store and the lot.

Compare this to a convenience store that is a large cinder block building with only a single glass door and maybe two smaller windows, most of it covered with advertisements. You cannot see what is happening inside and the clerk is not able to see outside. Both are convenience stores. However, because of the design the opportunity for crime increases significantly with little natural surveillance available.

Being aware of these design features can dramatically decrease your opportunity of becoming a crime victim. If you have a choice of an open parking garage over an enclosed structure, choose the open location for your safety. In the same manner, an open and well-lit convenience store will be less of a crime attractor to a criminal than one that would conceal a robbery from the outside. If you have a choice of locations on your daily travels, opt for the location that provides natural surveillance.

This makes if clear that by simply altering small things about either a location or your routine while there you can dramatically limit your risk of crime. Criminals are operating under bounded rationality, making reasonable calculations based on only what they know. They balance rewards and costs just like anyone else. Such decisions are universal. **They are more likely to avoid immediate and credible threats more than distant and non-credible threats**. Therefore, you need to be aware of locations and situations that benefit the bad guys. **Avoiding an alert victim is more of a deterrent to a criminal than the unlikely event of going to jail.**

Although a city may be high in crime the crime is almost always localized to only a few very distinct areas. However, there are certain indicators that there will be a higher probability of finding these crime hot spots. **Neighborhoods of single-family homes that are owner occupied have significantly less crime than neighborhoods that are primarily single-family homes occupied by renters. And neighborhoods filled with renters are far less likely to have crime than neighborhoods filled with a large number of apartment complexes.**

In the next chapter we will go into greater detail about this, but this occurs for two primary reasons. **Private space that is cared for decreases the opportunity for crime because someone is watching out for the location. Secondly, ownership increases a person's ties to a community, making them less likely to engage in any criminal behavior that might harm what they have built.** Renters, particularly those in apartment complexes, are far more transitory and have much less to lose if they commit a crime.

In addition to the concept of private space we will look at how changes in design can affect the risks that your home might present. Often simple steps such as the removal of crannies and corners and brighter spaces offer low cost measures to decrease the risk of crime.

SECURING YOUR HOME

Environmental Design:

The typical residential burglar is looking for the greatest reward for the least amount of risk. He will weigh his risks and look for the best opportunity to avoid being caught. Home invaders have a slightly different objective. They too are looking for the greatest reward with the least amount of risk, but now their reward involves taking control over those in a residence. Burglars rely on stealth and prefer an empty home, while home invaders want something from those inside the house and will gain entry by deception or extreme force.

Whether you are dealing with a property crime or a physical assault the vast majority of criminals will operate from a rational perspective. Like anyone else, and perhaps even more so, criminals will look for the easiest target, even if the payoff is less. Unlike the different businesses and locations you go to throughout your day, you can make strides to improve the security of your own property. All you have to realize is that **criminals look for the easiest targets over the greater payoff**. Understanding this allows you to visualize your property from the perspective of a potential burglar and take steps to increase the difficulty of accessing the property.

The idea of creating defensible space through design was developed by Oscar Newman in the early 1970s. It has gone on to become known as Crime Prevention Through Environmental Design (CPTED). Newman's concepts developed after watching Pruitt-Igoe, a state of the art, 2,740 unit low income housing development rapidly fall into disrepair and become overrun with crime. It was marketed as the future of low-income housing when it was built. Instead it was torn down in less than a decade after becoming a plight to St. Louis. In the shadow of Pruitt-Igoe was an older development of row houses that catered to the same low income, single parent families. It suffered none of the crime issues of its neighbor and remained fully occupied during the same decade, even though it sat directly across the street from Pruitt-Igoe. What Newman recognized about the differences in the two developments was the importance of ownership and private space in the prevention of crime. His ideas led to four basic principles of achieving defensible space known as territoriality, natural surveillance, image, and milieu.

Territoriality implies the development of a sense of ownership of your property. **The more you can define your private space the better. When a location has too much public space it loses a sense of control and gives an offender the idea that he could belong there.**

To put this in the simplest form, compare two houses. One sits feet from the sidewalk, where another sits a hundred yards off the street and has two large pillars at the end of the drive. In the first situation an offender could explain his reason for being near a person's property because it's difficult to know where private property ends and public space begins. However, it's difficult to explain why the same guy is 50 yards into a property that has clearly defined pillars at the end of the drive. **Just the mere fact that an offender can't justify why he is somewhere can offer a deterrent effect on his decisions.**

Obviously this is an extreme example, but it's used to illustrate the idea of Territoriality. And it is not dependent on eliminating access, but in defining the space as personal space. In a practical sense, a fence around a property, a row of bushes, signs, or even lighting can be used to define a space. **The simple act of defining the space as being separate from others and under some ownership gives a** criminal a psychological sense of the boundaries. **By crossing these boundaries he already knows he's in violation and has fewer viable excuses to explain why he is there.**

This can clearly be seen in a study conducted of thefts from autos by the British Home Office. **A car parked on the street in front of a house is 3 times as likely to be broken into as a car parked in the home's driveway (Mirlees-Black, et al, 1996). Although the cars may only be sitting a few yards apart, the car in the street is in a public space while the driveway is a defined private space. This makes the criminal's excuses for being there more difficult. That simple psychological barrier is important and should be maximized.**

Territoriality can also be implemented by limiting access to only those that have a right to be on the property. In a high rise this can be accomplished by a keypad entry on an automatically shutting front door or by the presence of a doorman. This can work well in apartment buildings that can afford such features, but this is often unavailable in low-income high rises. In the case of Pruitt-Igoe there was no limit to accessing the buildings and each building had multiple large areas meant for the people living in the apartments to use as shared space. But no one maintained these areas. This meant that each tenant thought that the responsibility for caring for the area was on someone else. With no one caring for the locations they soon became overrun with drug addicts and dealers, ultimately making the residence feel trapped in their own apartments.

That's why it makes sense to limit access to any property. This can be accomplished with something like a guardhouse at the entrance of a parking lot. Even if the guardhouse is never occupied its mere presence makes it clear that this area is off limits to all but those that live in a community. An unoccupied guardhouse gives the impression that a guard is on duty and patrolling the property. It doesn't matter that a guard never worked at the location. Criminals make a rational decision, based on limited information, that a guardhouse implies a guard is somewhere nearby.

Taken to a larger area we can see the impact of Territoriality over streets or neighborhoods. Limiting the number of entrances to a neighborhood directly affects the amount of crime that will occur there. The more heavily travelled the road a house sits on, the more potential for burglary and theft you face. It's not just from the mere presence of more people, but it also applies to the idea that a main road is a public space, where a dead end road into a subdivision is viewed as private.

This makes it clear that if you have the option between a house on a through street and one on a cul-de-sac, the property on the cul-de-sac will generally be a better choice for security reasons. A criminal realizes that most of the cars on a cul-de-sac belong to the residents. Those residents are also more likely to see a car that seems out of place. On the other hand, a car parked on a street that has a mix of use between businesses and residential won't draw any undue attention as cars come and go from the area frequently. No one is likely to be suspicious of a new car to the area as it is something that happens everyday. In addition, a cul-de-sac only offers one means of escape if traveling by car. A through street allows for multiple means of leaving the scene to avoid the police.

Natural surveillance - how well can occupants see their surroundings and how well can neighbors do the same. Privacy certainly has its benefits, but it does tend to increase an offender's perception of safety at the same time. The fewer bushes and alcoves directly surround a building, the fewer opportunities criminals have at remaining hidden from view.

Image - refers to the ability of a building's design to influence the perception of an area as unique, well maintained, and non-isolated. In essence you want your property to look like someone cares. This is related to the Broken Windows Theory, that once a building has a broken window, if it isn't soon replaced, a sense that no one cares will develop and more windows will be broken. This leads to more crimes being committed and eventually more violent crimes.

This can happen at both an individual building level or at a neighborhood level. As more houses go into disrepair a whole block can take on a sense of no one is watching, leading to a decrease in safety to all the residents. This is clearly scene in Detroit where more and more homes were abandoned; leaving those that remained with little reason to maintain their own property as their houses are rapidly losing value. Within a short time such neighborhoods become the playground for illicit behavior because there is no one left to stop it.

Image really comes down to taking ownership over what is yours. By caring for the property, cleaning up trash, making repairs, you are not just taking care of the property, but decreasing the chance that it will be victimized. This is really seen clearly in neighborhoods that are largely rental properties when compared to neighborhoods filled with owners. By having an ownership interest in a property it is more likely to be maintained. Renters don't feel the same obligation. Unfortunately, this also increases their risks. The difference in crime rates between neighborhoods that are rental properties and single-family owners can be dramatic, even if only separated by a street.

This idea ties into the remaining principle, known as Milieu. This involves the positioning of a property within its surrounding area. Simply stated, a place will be safe if it's surrounded by safe places. Such locations find it easier to keep the spillover of crime out.

A neighborhood or home that is situated near a rundown neighborhood will be in an area known as an edge. Such areas tend to be high in crime because they are areas where criminals feel comfortable as they are near home and do not appear out of place. An edge also provides for an ample amount of victims that tend to be more affluent and less suspicious. From a criminal's perspective it becomes the perfect location for crime. This type of area is most easily understood as the five or six blocks immediately around a college campus in a major city. Here you expect to see both college students and inner city people going to and from their classes or homes. This makes it a target rich environment.

Once you understand the concepts of territoriality, natural surveillance, image, and milieu you can begin to implement a plan of building a defensible space around yourself and your property. In the following chapter, we'll look at some of the steps you can take to make your home into a hard target.

CPTED PRINCIPLES INTO PRACTICE

To build a psychological wall of protection around your property, you need to be aware of what are the easiest points of entry that allow for the least amount of natural surveillance from neighbors. A high rear fence may allow for a nice private yard for a Sunday afternoon, but also allows the necessary concealment for a burglar to operate without being noticed.

Recognize that bushes can provide cover to a willing criminal. Keep bushes well groomed to show concern for the property while still limiting concealment for an offender. Bushes and plants at the edge of your property act as a natural barrier to define your private space, but bushes should be removed from around points of entry where they offer cover near windows and doors. The only useful plants around windows are prickly plants, such as a holly or a rose bush, that act as a natural deterrent as no one wants to be poked or cut in the process of a crime.

Are windows open and doors unlocked? Such simple measures as locking doors are all too often overlooked, particularly when you are home. The only reason a burglar might target a residence is being able to see a door or window clearly left open. It reveals itself as an easy opportunity, even if there is very little of value inside. When you are home, only the windows that require substantial effort by an intruder to enter should be open, and doors should never be left unlocked whether you are home or away. **Both locked doors and windows are the first line of defense against both property crime and physical violence. Simply locking doors buys time. Half of all burglaries would be prevented if a door had not been left unlocked.** This fact does not put blame on the victims. We all want to be able to trust our neighbors and expect a certain amount of respect for our property. But it's important to see that criminals are unwilling to put too much time into anything, hence the reason they become criminals. We shouldn't make their job any easier. Each additional kick at a door increases the potential for a burglar to draw attention to himself, thus decreasing the likelihood of him risking entering a home. **Criminals look for opportunity and avoid effort.**

Doors act like a knight's shield, providing protection against an initial assault. As soon as that door is open, you expose yourself to a threat. Windows near the door or a peephole are necessities before you decide to remove that shield to a potential threat. However, glass panes in doors or beside doors that can be smashed and allow a criminal to reach in and throw both a door lock and a deadbolt will be seen as opportunities and not barriers. If your door has windows, or is within arm's reach of a window, think seriously about installing a double cylinder deadbolt that requires a key on both the interior and exterior. If the window is smashed, the burglar will be no better off, as long as the key is not left in the lock for your own convenience. A key can certainly be left nearby, just out of arms reach from the window.

A weapon should be available within your arm's length of an open door. Anything beyond arm's length makes you unarmed. The weapon doesn't need to be a gun or knife, but something that can give a mechanical advantage over an opponent and offer a form of intimidation. A golf club hardly meets that criteria, but a Louisville Slugger will do nicely.

In terms of using CPTED principles to their maximum in such circumstance, you wouldn't put a ball bat against the door with the obvious guise that it is there as a weapon. If you put an antique baseball bat, old glove, and a weathered baseball sitting next to the door you have added a simple antique sports décor to your home. The benefit is that the bat could immediately be used to defend yourself with no one knowing it was there for that purpose.

Chain locks on doors offer little in the way of deterrence. Once a door is open the three or four inches of the chain, a simple push of body weight will pull the screws holding the lock from the door or frame. If you are not expecting sudden force against the door, you will be unable to keep an offender from forcing their way in. On the other hand, a simple rubber doorstopper placed on the floor, allowing the door to open a few inches, can prevent even a determined criminal from gaining entry by force. The more force exerted, the more the stopper will be forced into the floor.

At night, the more lighting you can give your property the better. Lighting designates your private space, making it difficult for a criminal to explain why he is there. This makes it a highly effective deterrent at night. Shadows and cover are a prowler's best friends. You want to decrease any such opportunities by casting as much light as reasonable.

Motion activated lights in particular are effective because they create an immediate psychological reaction in a criminal that he may have just been spotted. A burglar cannot be certain if he'd been seen or if he merely activated the light. This leads to expectations that the police have been called or that a shotgun is being racked. To a criminal acting rationally, this is an opportunity to flee rather than risk an alert homeowner.

If you have a ladder that is too long to place in the garage it is all too often left alongside the house. Such a ladder is only an open invitation to a criminal and offers good access to second story windows that may be shut, but not locked. Such ladders need to be locked securely to a tree or other permanent object to prevent them being used against your own best interest.

You should try to examine your house during both the day and the night to have a good understanding of what a burglar might see as a weak point. What you are looking for are the easiest routes to enter your home that offer the least opportunity to be observed. Once you determine what a criminal might consider a weak point it becomes relatively simple to set out to harden those entrances.

As you examine your property start at the furthest point out and work your way in. You want the first challenge to a criminal to be the furthest from you and your family. This is at the outer perimeter of your property. Ideally this would involve a gated fence that will keep out all but the most motivated offender and send them looking for another target.

Realistically, not everyone has the luxury of such a set up. However, motion detectors at the end of the driveway do allow for advanced warning. If a knock comes at the door and the detector did not warn you in advance, you have the benefit of having elevated suspicion about who is at the door.

Implementing some simple design element at the edge of the property from trees, bushes, flowerbeds, fencing, posts can all go to make your home more secure. Unlike a gate that physically stops a suspect from entering by requiring some form effort to enter, these are merely psychological barriers that act more as stop signs to warn someone they are coming onto private space. Once they cross this point they have to be able to explain why they are there. Even making a criminal explain why he is somewhere he shouldn't be is enough to convince him to move elsewhere.

Inner Perimeter

With the benefit of technology, Closed Circuit Television (CCTV) that was once limited by cost to businesses only a few years ago are now routinely available to almost everyone. Wireless systems require very little to set up and allow for both daytime and nighttime surveillance. The principle purpose of CCTV is to record an event so that it can be used to catch a criminal and then to get a conviction. A CCTV with monitors also allows you to see what may be happening around your property without exposing yourself to risk. However, your primary goal is to prevent a crime from occurring. To a burglar, the knowledge that he might be watched is his biggest fear. It gives him the sense that he will be caught in the act and poses an immediate, tangible threat.

You can play on that psychological knowledge in two ways with CCTV. First, you can post signs that the premises are under 24-hour surveillance. You are merely warning a possible intruder that he is being watched. In a similar fashion, a simple alarm sign posted near the front entrance has a similar deterrent effect. Professional signs can be bought online or at hardware stores for a few dollars, making the psychological benefit of monitored security available to almost anyone for fewer than twenty dollars.

Dummy cameras that pivot and have a flashing light can be bought for fewer than ten dollars. Although these cameras can't be used to make a case against a criminal, they achieve your primary objective, which is crime prevention. A burglar is looking for an easy target. You want your home to appear to be too much effort and to much risk. Some people fear that such actions merely move the criminal next door. However, this is rarely the case. Once a criminal perceives that one house has security, it increases his suspicions that other houses nearby have security. This creates a diffusion of benefits to neighbors, rather than making them more vulnerable.

The important thing is to not make cameras covert. You're not trying to catch a nanny misbehaving with a camera hidden in a clock. You want a criminal to perceive that there is a risk. This is the only way to deter their actions. A uniformed police officer is more of a deterrent to crime than an undercover officer. In fact, an undercover officer might be acting as bait for a robber or a thief. He wants just the opposite of deterrence. In a similar fashion, you want your security to be obvious to prevent crime. At night, the flashing red light of a dummy camera will be quite obvious at a distance and cause a criminal to think twice before attempting to break in.

You can also play on the psychological fears of a criminal with a few other signs. A Gadsden "Don't Tread on Me," flag, a marine simper fi, or an US flag have similar meanings to anyone that sees them. Each flag conveys a message of independence and belong to those people most likely to be prepared to defend what is theirs without having to say it directly.

Just the opposite is also true. It is all too common to see a business that posts a No CCW sticker on the door being robbed a day or two after the sign is put on the door. Signs that state No concealed weapons do not deter crime, they openly invite it. When James Holmes went on a shooting spree in Aurora, Colorado, he was looking for the greatest number of people he could shoot and kill. He made his decision on what movie theater to target by avoiding those closer to him and went specifically to the theater that had a No CCW sticker posted. He ended up killing 12 and wounding 70 because he knew he would not face any opposition. **When your intent is to commit a crime, you are looking for the easiest opportunity to commit that crime with the least amount of risk.**

A beware of dog sign and a large dog bowl and chain near the door are useful devices. Even more devious is a handwritten note stuck to the door that says, "Dan, the damn Raccoon got into the house again! I'm not going back in until you find him!"

Would you go in that house? I would guess probably not. Neither would a criminal. It doesn't matter that no one named Dan lives in your home or that you never had a problem with Raccoons. You are merely playing a mind game against someone looking for the least amount of risk.

One additional marking you want for your residence is for the street address to be clearly identifiable from the road. If you need assistance, whether from the police or from the fire department, you want that assistance to find you as soon as possible. Clear address markings at the curb and on the house decrease unnecessary delays in getting help as the police or firefighters search for the right house.

This is equally important in apartment buildings. Apartments need to be clearly marked and make logical sense to someone who has never set foot in the building. Most cops and paramedics have had the experience of going past apartment 1, 2, 3 and then stumbling into apartment 9 for no apparent reason. It makes it very difficult to get much help if you're in apartment 5 if no one can find it.

Entry points

Lock your doors whether you are home or away. Make sure to use deadbolts, preferably double cylinder locks that require a key on both the inside and outside. Reinforce strike plates on the doorjamb by inserting three inch screws rather than the one and half inch screws that typically come with the lock.

Realize that the total strength of your door is dependent on the strength of a two-inch piece of metal sticking into rather soft wood. One strong kick is enough to overwhelm most doors. That's largely because the force of a kick is directed against the lock which then simply cuts through the wood on the inside of the door jam. The addition of longer screws helps to allow the metal strike plate to be secured not just by the door jam, but also to the stud in the frame behind it.

To make a door significantly more secure, and with very little cost, you can reinforce the door by prying the interior door trim away and reinforcing the jamb with additional wood and a metal mending plate. With the jamb removed, you can see that the doorframe has a gap between it and the stud. A piece of thin wood slid into this gap allows the screws in the strike plate to have more to bite into. You can then reinforce this by screwing a metal mending plate over the doorjamb. A seven to ten inch metal mending plate that is no wider than the trim piece can be screwed into the side of the door jam. Mending plates have multiple screw holes, allowing for four or more screws to be driven in above and below both the doorknob and the deadbolt. You may need to chisel away some wood to let the plate sit flush, but once your done, the trim can be reinstalled with no one being the wiser that the lock has been beefed up. A kick against this stronger doorframe will make even repeated kicks far less effective at defeating the lock.

Stepping the defensive measures up another step is to have exterior doors that swing outward. Such doors are uncommon in most areas, but in hurricane zones they are often part of building codes. Hurricane force winds can blow through inward opening doors, but not an outward opening door. In a similar fashion, a criminal will have much more difficulty attempting to pull open a door than kicking through it. However, the hinges are on the outside, making it imperative that the hinges are designed so the pins cannot be pried out with a screwdriver.

As discussed earlier, motion activated lights near entrances have both a deterrent effect and allow for visibility for you and your neighbors if placed near your doors.

If you have a sliding door, make sure to have some form of block beyond the latch built into the door. These locks are generally flimsy at best, and often require little more than a flathead screwdriver to pry loose. A simple dowel rod or PVC pipe in the track can prevent the door from sliding if the lock is forced. Make sure the rod has a large enough diameter that the door cannot be lifted over it.

Interior

Make potential weapons available to you in any room you may find yourself. You don't have to think in terms of guns or knives scattered around the house, although it's possible. However, a bat or similar item that you can instinctively go to and know it is available is critical in a panic situation. As we will cover later, in high stress situations your body and mind tend to go into a total lockdown. Trying to improvise weapons when faced with an immediate threat is unlikely to happen. And there's no guarantee of the quality of a MacGyver device grabbed in a panic. By having a well-placed weapon that you can quickly get to no matter where you are in your home helps you have both a mechanical advantage over an opponent, but also creates a plan of what to do in any given event. **Advanced plans help you gain control in out of control situations.**

Safe Rooms

It is a worthwhile investment to consider having a specific room of the house designed to prevent an aggressive attack. It may not be a location that you find shelter for a prolonged event, but rather a room that allows you to buy time until help arrives.

With that thought in mind, the room has to have two key elements, both a highly defensible entry and a means of communication. The first step in creating a safe room is to replace the typical interior door with a solid wood or metal exterior door. The hinges must be on the interior of the room, so that an attacker cannot easily remove the hinge pin. Like your exterior doors, 3-inch screws should reinforce the strike plate, increasing the force necessary to knock the door from its frame. Also like your exterior doors, it should have a keyed doorknob and a deadbolt, rather than the simple locking knobs typically found on bedroom and bathroom doors.

The safe room location should also be difficult to access from the outside, but can provide escape from the inside. A second story room with a window that would allow you to call for help, while limiting an intruder's access to you is worth considering. Such a room should have a means of safely getting to the ground from inside, whether it is a simple knotted rope or a rope ladder.

You need a means of communication to get help. With a window this is relatively simple, otherwise keep your cellphone in the room is a simple step, particularly if that room is part of your normal routine as you get ready in the morning. Such a place is not an out of the way place where you are likely to forget your phone when you leave and is readily accessible when you need it. A landline phone or a Wi-Fi based device can also be left in the room. However, realize that phone lines and networks can easily be disabled. An emergency cell phone with no monthly plan simply left in its charger in the room is a reasonable alternative.

In general, a full sized bathroom makes for a good location. It allows for access to fresh water, walls filled with copper pipes, and the shelter of a tub. If you need access to Band-Aids or medicines they will be readily at hand. Reinforcing a door where you take a daily shower, and therefore are at your most vulnerable, also makes basic sense from a practical standpoint. Whether you ever need to retreat to the safety of such a room or not, the knowledge that the door is reinforced when you are about your daily activities will give you a sense of wellbeing that you wouldn't get from creating a special room out of a closet or somewhere in the basement that is rarely used.

The room should also house a weapon or two that can provide additional defense should the door be forced. Following Gibbs' Rule #9 from NCIS, "Never go anywhere without a knife," Most knives are inexpensive and easily concealed anywhere.

CPTED GUIDELINES

- Increase natural surveillance of the property. The more you can see the less comfortable a criminal becomes. You can accomplish this by increasing lighting, adding even imitation CCTV, or cutting plants back from windows.
-Define public and private space around your property. The more you can make your private property separate from those that surround it by defining it with small shrubs, fences, pillars, etc. the better.
-Don't display your valuables. A large picture window allows a prowler the opportunity to see not only what you have inside, but also get a good understanding of the layout of your house. The less he can see inside your property the less he will be tempted. He will also be less comfortable entering into an unknown space.
-Create an Image that gives a clear sense of pride and ownership. The less a property is kept up, the more likely it is to be victimized.

SITUATIONAL CRIME PREVENTION

Throughout your daily activity you want to decrease your vulnerability to crime by decreasing criminal opportunity. The primary things that a criminal looks for are defined as the things most CRAVED. These items are easily Concealable, Removable, Available, Valuable, Enjoyable and Disposable (Clarke, 1999).

The perfect example of a CRAVED item is a cell phone or a tablet. This type of item is easily hidden by a thief, requires little effort to take, they are readily available, can represent hundreds of dollars of value, are central to most people's entertainment, and can be easily sold off for cash.

Such items represent one of the most common items taken from autos, homes, or simply taken off of people. In 2013 it's estimated that 3.1 million mobile devices were stolen. To decrease the opportunity for a thief to take such items we can address the issue through Situational Crime Prevention.

Situational Crime Prevention relies on five general categories as defined by researchers Clarke and Cornish (2003) to decrease opportunities for crime. These crime prevention actions are increasing effort, increasing risk, reducing the reward, reducing provocations, and removing excuses. We will cover each individually to try to better understand how they can be implemented in your daily routine.

One approach to decrease the opportunity for theft is by increasing the effort to acquire an item. A highly craved item left visible in a vehicle, left on a table, or one that you are actively using, but are unaware of your surroundings, offers little to deter a criminal. It has become quite common to simply take a phone from someone who is actively texting, or watching videos. This is known as Apple Picking. Users of cell phones become so caught up in the device that they are completely unaware of the environment and the people around them.

To decrease the opportunity, you must increase the risk of being caught. If you leave a mobile device or a backpack, even for a moment, it becomes very tempting to a thief. He will rationalize that the device doesn't mean much to whoever left it, but it will readily meet his immediate needs or wants. Leaving such items out in the open, even within a locked car, only invites criminal behavior.

You simply cannot walk away from such items, or they will walk away from you. If you leave a tablet on a table to go to the bathroom ask someone to watch the item. Although not recommended, this even works by asking a stranger sitting next to you to watch your item. The act of drawing his attention to you and the tablet makes him aware that the item is yours. Otherwise someone could walk up and take the item and the person sitting next to you would have no clue that the item just walked off.

In a similar fashion, instead of leaving a cell phone sitting in a locked car on the seat, move it to the glove box or other area where it cannot be seen. With no guarantee that there is anything of value in the car, the risks of breaking in are not outweighed by the value of the property inside. This is the out of sight out of mind argument at its finest.

It is important to recognize that a criminal only sees something that he THINKS is valuable. It doesn't really matter what it is. A cell phone might be traded for 20 bucks or a gram of crack cocaine. It doesn't matter the item's real value, it only feeds an immediate need for a thief. A diaper bag left in your car, in the mind of the thief, might contain DVDs, a wallet, or a camera. You know it's nothing of value, but the thief, is acting only under bounded rationality. He has limited information, but it's rational for him to believe that something of value is in that bag. He will think nothing of breaking a window and taking off with ten dollars of diapers and baby wipes, only to drop it around the corner when he sees it has nothing of value. Now you're out the time for repairs, money, and stuck with a stinky baby if he's a mess when you get back to the car.

There have been cases where criminals have run up and grabbed a bag off a person casually walking their dog, only to find he's made off with a bag full of poop. **The ease of the opportunity completely outweighs the value of the item.**

A third approach to reducing crime is to reduce the reward to the offender. One of the simplest innovations to decrease the value of cell phones and tablets is to have a kill switch installed in the operating system. If the device is stolen, it simply becomes inoperable to the thief. This essentially takes the value out of the property and decreases its attractiveness to offenders. After such programs are installed, knowledge of it spreads quickly among the criminal element.

In New York City, robberies of Apple products fell 19 percent after kill switches were made available on OS while thefts of Android phones without kill switches increased 40 percent. San Francisco saw similar results with iPhone robberies dropping 38 percent, while robberies of Samsung devices increased 12 percent.

A fourth approach is decreasing provocations. This means limiting stressful situations that might lead to criminal activity. Flaunting or bragging about an item only makes it more desirable. This can frustrate someone who knows they don't have the ability to acquire a similar item on their own.

An example of this was a kid walking near an inner city park with an iPhone 6 only weeks after it was first released. 15 kids attacked the victim while he played with his new toy. They took off with the phone before the victim even knew what happened. He could have just as well been walking along with a handful of hundreds and run less risk.

A fifth approach is to remove any excuses for the behavior. Criminals have a remarkable ability to justify their actions based on what the victim does, or quickly deny that they even know something is against the law. You remove excuses by make it clear that something is wrong. A cell phone left out on a table allows a criminal to justify taking it by thinking, "Well, it wasn't important to them. They must not want it. Otherwise, why just leave it out?" However, if the phone is behind a counter in a private area, it makes it difficult for the criminal to explain why they are there.

Let's move up in size from cell phones to automobiles. This will show how simple steps all but eliminate the opportunity for a crime to occur. Each year cops expect auto thefts to begin to spike in the winter. There is one simple explanation for this. As the weather turns cold people leave their cars running as they dash into the store to grab a newspaper or a coffee. "I'll only be a second," is the thought that has led to many a stranded motorist.

Good people find it difficult to think that someone would take something of theirs and that it can happen so quickly. A criminal doesn't think about you. A criminal only sees an immediate opportunity to get out of the cold and get to where he's going. He sees absolutely no risk in taking a running car. He gets the immediate adrenaline rush of taking the item, while being completely aware that it will take a minute for the victim to know what happened, two or three minutes for the dispatcher to report the crime to police, and probably 8 minutes for the police to arrive at the scene. By the time the victim is talking to police, the suspect has already wrecked or dumped the car and is merrily on about his day.

Knowing that the leading cause of auto thefts is the victim leaving the keys in the car is what brings Situational Crime Prevention clearly into light. **If you are doing something that makes things convenient for you, you have just made things equally convenient to a criminal.** Carrying large sums of cash, leaving doors unlocked, leaving your tablet on the table as you run to the bathroom, trusting a Nigerian prince who just needs your bank account so he can send you a large sum of money, are all just opportunities for a criminal.

Situational Crime Prevention requires that you define the specific crime you want to address to help create the means of stopping the behavior. Once you define the crime you must determine **what is a criminal willing to do to get that item?** Once you know that, you can set up a means of preventing his actions. Generally, the steps will be simple, but are done with the specific idea of preventing a specific crime. You have to realize a criminal will react more impulsively and have a higher tolerance for risk than you do. However, when you realize that criminals act rationally then you can take simple steps to increase the effort and risk of committing a crime while reducing the reward and the excuses for the behavior.

Let's take one last look at situational crime prevention to see how simple it is to implement. In an earlier chapter I discussed the idea of a crime generator. It's the type of location that generates crime simply because it offers so much opportunity. The parking lot of a large community park with a beach or a walking trail is a prime example of a crime generator, particularly in a tourist area. A criminal knows that the people in the lot are likely to be away from their car for a period of time. They are likely to be travelling with a lot of items in their cars that are valuable. If he spots an intended victim who is running, biking, or going for a swim he knows that she is likely to keep her valuables in the car, rather than to be weighed down by the items as she runs. Even worse, the unwitting victim will often reveal that there is something valuable in the car by popping the rear door of her SUV and throwing a purse in the back to 'secure' it.

Although SUVs have made life convenient by allowing us to carry more things, their downside is the rear door is not nearly as secure as a conventional trunk. The most common crime cops see in a parking lot of a recreation center is a smashed out rear window in an SUV. The criminal just sat and watched for the first person to toss her valuables in the back and waited for the opportune time to break the rear window and make off with the property. **If your going to hide something in your car, hide it before your arrive at your destination. Otherwise, you are merely advertising to a criminal that you have something of value and exactly where it is.**

This is even more imperative in a tourist area where the criminal has the benefit of knowing that even if he is caught the victim is unlikely to show up for court. All thief has to do to lower his risk is target out of state plates. If he's caught he might serve a night or two in jail, but his case will be tossed out for want of prosecution because the victim is back home and 1000 miles away by the time the case goes to trial. Tourist areas are target rich environments - Low risk, high reward. As you can see, the idea of being arrested or serving any significant time would not be seen as a significant risk to a criminal in such an area. It is up to you to take a specific action that can prevent the crime from occurring.

ROBBERY

The two boys rounded the corner with robbery on their mind. The victim knew that they were up to no good as soon as he saw them. He turned and felt himself tense up and speed his steps to his car. Perhaps he was just prejudging them, or so he reasoned, up until the moment they pushed him against his Lexus and placed the Beretta nervously only a few inches from his face.

Officers got the call and were on scene only minutes after the event at 11 o'clock at night. However, the staging for that event had been building for over six hours. Two customers sitting on the front porch of the restaurant near where the robbery happened saw the two boys milling around in the area in front of the business around 5pm. The boys were not doing anything overtly bad, but they simply seemed to be hanging out without any real reason to be there. Both customers knew that something about the boys was wrong and even discussed it between each other. Even though they sensed it, they dismissed it.

A restaurant employ took garbage out around 9pm and saw the boys standing in the alcove of the business next door. It wasn't raining, or overly hot, so there was no reason to seek shelter there. The boys were just hanging out in the alcove of a closed business. The employee knew there was something about the two boys, but didn't say anything or call the cops.

So, at 11pm, the owner of the business heads out to his car unaware of a potential threat. As soon as he left the building the boys came running around the front of the restaurant, where the two customers had first seen them. The restaurant owner immediately knew that they were up to no good. He braced himself to be hit because he assumed it was going to be a knock out game. His reaction was to first look over his shoulder, while turning and walking away from them quickly towards his car. He raised his shoulders, slumped his head, hoping to take the brunt of whatever physical attack was to come on his shoulders and back, rather than his head. However, instead of coming up and punching him in the head, one jabbed a gun at him and demanded everything he had. They made off with a cell phone and a pack of cigarettes. The old saying is true - crime doesn't pay.

Four people at three separate times saw these boys and immediately understood that something about them was intrinsically wrong. The first two sensed it, but dismissed it, perhaps out of political correctness. Both witnesses felt guilty of not doing something about it after the robbery occurred, knowing that if they had simply called the police because the boys were suspicious the kids would have realized they had lost their opportunity and left the area.

This one event reveals so many elements of a classic robbery and how to avoid it. We look at the event from all of the elements that we've examined up to this point.

The first issue was the age of the boys. They were described as being between 17 and 20 years old, placing them squarely in the age range most likely to engage in criminal or risky behavior. Deviant behavior spikes during this timeframe, only to desist in most people by the age of 28.

The second element is the fact that there were two suspects. As Ration Choice Theory explains, two adolescent boys will tend to drive each other to deviant behavior out of peer pressure, each reinforcing the stupid decision of the other. They also gain increased confidence as they rationalize that the two of them could easily overpower a single victim. In many ways, criminals are like the cast of

Jackass, only looking to hurt others rather than each other.

The fact that the suspects were both boys also increased the risk factor. Official reports such as the Uniform Crime Report indicate that males commit 80% of crimes. Official records show that men lead in all criminal behavior by a significant margin in all but prostitution and embezzlement, two crimes where women feel forced into by economic stress. Edwin Sutherland (1949) was the first to show with his Sex Role Theory the clear gender differences that lead to more crime in boys. Sutherland saw a strong correlation between how boys are socialized that led to increased deviancy. He saw that girls are more likely to be supervised than boys, while boys were more likely to be encouraged to take risks and be aggressive.

The location of the crime is also central to how and why the crime occurred. The restaurant itself was located in an exclusive, upscale neighborhood, filled with high-end boutiques, art stores, and trendy restaurants. A couple blocks to the West are million dollar homes that are enormous, turn of the century marble and stone mansions. Two blocks to the North are homes that are filled with ornate woodwork, heavy pocket doors, stained-glass windows from a bygone era, but little chance that the property could ever be sold for over forty thousand dollars. This area was once the home to middle class workers that commuted only a couple miles to downtown. Those people have long since moved to the suburbs. Now the neighborhood is an area of extreme poverty, with only a few homeowners remaining.

Ernest Burgess (1925) defined this type of area as a Zone of Transition, an area around the city center where workers lived until they were able to move to more stable neighborhoods. This type of neighborhood was first used to describe Chicago, but is common throughout most large Eastern and Midwest cities. People that could move out of this area, whether they were Black or White, did so as soon as they could afford to do so. That left only those without the ability and resources to leave the neighborhood stuck in an environment that was slowly decaying. The Zone of Transition is the location where you are most likely to see the highest amount of criminal behavior. In most major cities this area encircles the city center just outside the Central Business District. In general, each neighborhood that places you further out from the Central Business District tends to lead to more affluence and less crime.

In this case, the Zone of Transition sits within a few blocks of a significant amount of old wealth; the type of wealth that doesn't move, even as the area around it changes. As mentioned in the chapter on Place, this type of area is defined as an Edge where two different environments meet. The six or so blocks immediately around that Edge run a high risk of crime because both those that are well to do and those that are in extreme poverty are both expected to be in that area. Such a combination of the haves and have-nots makes for good opportunities for those with criminal intentions because they know the area well, they are close to the security of home, and the chance for a good payoff are greater.

The robbery happened in mid-May, just as the weather was improving and more people were out enjoying the chance to be out after a long, cold winter. As the weather improved, the Routine Activities of both the criminals and the victims changed. The robbers were out because they knew their opportunity to run into someone out by themselves would increase with the warmer weather.

The two robbers carefully waited in the right location for a suitable victim. The employee carrying out trash by herself two hour before may have been an easy target, but offered little reward for the effort.

However, the owner of the business, walking to his Lexus, appeared to be both an easy target and likely to be worth the risk.

If so many physical crimes play out in a similar fashion, what can be done to prevent the crime from occurring? We will take situational crime prevention we looked at in the last chapter for property crime and use it for personal defense.

AWARENESS

The greatest victory is that which requires no battle. - Sun Tzu

The robbery event I described brings us to one of the most important aspects of crime prevention - awareness. Multiple people saw the same two boys, all felt uneasy about them and their behavior, and all dismissed it.

At least the victim and witnesses were even cognizant of the world around them. **Modern technology has given us the ability to constantly be in contact with the outside world, without being aware of the world around us.**

Dom Raso served 12 years in the SEAL teams. His number one piece of advice for self-defense is, "Get your head out of your phone." People simply are so plugged into Twitter, Facebook, email, and YouTube that they quite literally no longer experience their own environment. From the context of a criminal looking for an easy target, what could be better?

A person stuck in their phone is someone walking around carrying several hundred dollars worth of technology with no idea of what is happening around them. This total lack of awareness is what puts people into dangerous situations. They are blindly walking into criminal events that could be avoided if they simply paid attention to what's going on around them.

By being aware we can avoid bad situations all together. Raso advises to always remember, "Avoid, avoid, avoid. I want to avoid any situation before it happens." (Seidl, 2014). This sort of mindset means that you are thinking in terms of being prepared to get out of any bad situation. When you are in a room, are you aware of where the exits are? If you only know of the exit you came in, what if that's the entrance a mass shooter decides to use? How long will it take you to figure out an escape route under stress? If you are on the street, or at a friend's house, could you give the address to the police to get assistance without delay?

When you prepare for a flight you are instructed on the location of exits, oxygen masks, and floatation devices. Most of us are so familiar with the instructions that we ignore them. The instructions are to make you aware of the few things you can control in a crisis situation and yet they are often dismissed. This same attitude extends into our daily routines. It's important that we shake loose a mindset of complacency and become aware of warning signs and knowing what our options are if a situation turns critical.

To gain a better understanding of this we will look at preventing crime based on the color code of conditional awareness.

CONDITIONAL AWARENESS

Condition white, yellow, orange, red, and black

Lieutenant Colonel Jeff Cooper, the father of Modern Handgun Technique and founder of Gun site Training Center, clearly understood that surviving dangerous encounters was more dependent on an individual's mindset than on the skill set or weapon used. He knew and taught that both are important, but in developing your skills at arms you are also preparing yourself to evaluate situations that allow you to think tactically to avoid or win an encounter, rather than finding yourself at a tactical disadvantage.

It's unlikely that any police recruit could get through his first week of the academy without having Col. Cooper's color code drilled into their lower cerebellum. Each color designates a state of awareness and recruits are constantly reminded of the importance of remaining out of condition white when it comes to survival.

White is the state of utter disconnect from your surroundings. Like mentioned before, it's being completely engrossed in a text conversation on your cell phone where you could easily walk straight into a water fountain or bump into a tree that you are completely unaware of. Condition white seems to define people in our modern society. Surrounded by so many technological gizmos, and preoccupied with so many distractions most people are often completely clueless of their surroundings. Reality has taken a secondary place to a virtual world in many people's daily routines.

Condition white is defined by the relatively new crime known as Apple picking. When you are so focused on your device, you allow yourself to become an easy target. This combines both an opportunity with a highly CRAVED item. Thieves find it easy to simply run up and snatch a cell phone from an unsuspecting victim.

The first step in self-defense is to avoid condition white. It is a state that works well for sheep with a diligent shepherd nearby. It is dangerous to anyone else. The time to read a text, flip through a book, or watch a video is when you are behind a locked door. In condition white you feel completely secure and you are at your normal resting heart rate of 60-80 beats per minute (bpm). When you are out in public you are exposing yourself to any number of potential threats. You need to remain in condition yellow and alert to any potential threat.

Yellow is essentially the state you should operate in anytime you're outside of your locked home. In yellow you are aware of your surroundings, not completely caught off guard by anyone that might come within arm's reach of you. This is not a state of paranoia where you are always suspecting that someone is watching or following you. It is a state of alertness, expecting someone to be hiding in an alcove, around a corner, or behind a pillar. Such a state makes you take an added step away from such blind spots, buying yourself extra time and distance and taking opportunity away from a suspect. Rather than having your head down in a phone, you are consciously keeping your head up and shoulders back. Such a posture makes you appear more attentive, causing an offender to see you as a hard target compared to someone engrossed in a YouTube video. You are simply aware of your surroundings and ready to face any danger. Even so, your heart rate remains no different than condition white at 60-80 bpm.

The next stage is defined by the color orange. Orange is a stage where a threat has been perceived. Something about a situation or a person has caught your attention and caused you to take some preemptive action. This could be as simple as moving across the street to avoid a questionable person or as extreme as drawing a handgun to prepare for a potential confrontation. Due to the potential for confrontation, your body is beginning to send a surge of adrenaline to prepare for fight or flight. Your heart rate begins to elevate to 80-115 bpm.

At condition red you are actively engaged in physical action, whether it's punching, kicking or actively shooting. You are in full danger mode where your complex motor skills, visual reaction time, and cognitive reaction time are at their peak, but your fine motor skills are rapidly decreasing. Your heart rate may have doubled to 115-145 bpm.

The Marine Corp adapted a final color code that they define as black. Black designates a stage of mental shutdown. This generally occurs because a person in condition white is suddenly thrown violently into condition red. In condition black your heart rate surges to 175 bpm or higher while the level of oxygen to the brain begins to deplete. Vision and other senses begin to shut down. You have gone from a resting heart rate, to chest thumping beats that you can feel in your ears. The mind has shut down and the body freezes in fear, having no effective response to the circumstances it finds itself in. As you can imagine, this is a dangerous way to live. It is unlikely that you will, or can, make the proper decisions or carry out the actions to properly manage the situation. Freezing occurs because you simply have no response to the event as it unfolds.

This pattern of color codes helps to reveal the importance of remaining alert. By being in condition yellow when going about your daily activities you perceive threats and avoid them before they escalate. If you see something as a potential threat you can take some minor action that can prevent a situation from going to red. However, if you are oblivious to your surroundings, then you are likely to walk directly into an attack, decreasing your reaction time and eliminating almost all of your options. **Even if you are highly skilled with a handgun, have the gun on you, and it is a large enough caliber to stop a threat, you are still mentally unprepared to defend yourself if you are unaware.**

This is most clearly seen in the life and death of Wild Bill Hickok. A frontier lawman whose exploits became legendary, Hickok was one of the rare gunfighters who actually survived a classic, quick draw duel in the streets of Springfield, Missouri; The sort of image that later defined Western films. After his opponent, David Tutt, missed the lawman, Hickok calmly took aim with one hand and struck Tutt in the heart from 75 yards. This showed his remarkable skill with a handgun and his unwavering calm in the face of death. However, having survived a handful of other gunfights, Hickok was killed after sitting at a poker game with his back to the door. Jack McCall simply walked up behind Hickok and shot him pointblank in the back of the head. Wild Bill's skill and courage was no match for being ambushed from behind.

Today, many police officers that consciously choose to remain in condition yellow learn from the example of Wild Bill. When they sit in a restaurant, they place their back to a wall. They look up, if only for a second, to size up anyone that comes through the door to see if they pose a threat. Most cops do this instinctively off duty as well. In a similar fashion, police officers that are remaining in condition yellow have the windows of their cruisers cracked to hear what is going on outside their car as they patrol, trying to gain even a split second advantage as events unfold around them. When they pull up to a light, rather than pulling up next to the car beside them, they come to a stop slightly back from the other vehicle. This allows them to see the occupants of the car, but the driver would have to look over their shoulder to see, or take aim, at the officer. When responding to a call for service, alert officers pull up two or three houses away from where they are responding. This allows them to be out of the vehicle and able to access their weapon or seek cover if things turn deadly as they approach.

These basic principles can be applied to anyone's life by simply being aware of your surroundings. By remaining in condition yellow you are taking the first step in avoiding being thrown into a dangerous circumstance. If you are out and about, even with friends, and in an environment that you think is safe, it is worthwhile to remain alert no matter the circumstances.

Part of being aware is being conscious of when someone is entering your personal space. I'm sure you've met people who stand uncomfortably close to you during a conversation that made you feel ill at ease. It was likely someone elderly that is hard of hearing and perhaps not able to see that well, so they invade your natural comfort zone to carry on the conversation. But you naturally felt uncomfortable about them being that close.

In most circumstances that comfort zone is just out of arms reach. It's a natural recognition that we all have that realizes that to be harmed the other person has to take a step to grab or strike us. If someone enters your space and you take a step back to increase this personal space and the other person tries to close the distance, something isn't right.

In a dark parking lot with only a handful of cars, the comfort zone should be much greater. If a parking lot is the size of a football field and someone you don't know is trying to get within a few feet, something is very wrong.

In such a circumstance you need to take a deep breath, clinch your fists, and turn to address them while they are still more than three or four steps away.

A reasonable challenge question is, "What the fuck do you want?" This is the fine art of being bat shit crazy. This is a technical term to be sure, but one that clearly explains your objective. If the person has no ulterior motive, they will immediately back off, usually apologizing while they do. He'll go home thinking that lady is nuts. However, if the person is a predator he will have one of two reactions. He will immediately turn and leave because his perception of you as a victim has suddenly changed, or he will make a sudden attack. That's why you need to challenge at a distance. It gives you both time and distance to react.

Using coarse language is known as verbal stunning. Predators have a perception that their victims don't cuss. They view their victims as meek and timid. By using harsh language you can change a would-be attacker's perception of you as an easy target. Such an aggressive reaction shows that you might be a challenge, but requires no physical effort or skill on your part. Criminals rely on past experience that victim's don't make eye contact. Most victims will simply turn from the threat, hunch their shoulders, bury their head, and deny reality. **An aggressive reaction can stop a predator dead in his tracks due to it being so unexpected.**

This verbal threat might be enough to send a simple thief scurrying away. On the other hand, he may instead confront you and make it known that he wants money or something else of value. If he says, "give me the bag." Toss the bag one-way and head the other. Property is not worth fighting over and it sure is not worth losing your life.

However, if he simply rushes at you, by challenging him at a distance, you are buying a moment to react to his attack. You are under no obligation to allow him to swing first. The fact that you verbally confronted him and he continues is enough to indicate his intentions. As mentioned earlier, no one enters your personal space unnecessarily. Almost everyone has a natural sense to keep a stranger at arm's length. When someone violates this space outside of an elevator or a game of Twister you can justify striking out.

You have the right to defend yourself against physical harm, serious physical harm, and death. But you are not limited to that. You have the right to defend yourself against the **threat** of physical harm, serious physical harm, or death. If you fear for your safety, you need to act, not react. **Action almost always beats reaction.**

If you remain in condition yellow, you greatly decrease the opportunity for the threat to develop. You are not eliminating it, but significantly decreasing the chances that it can happen. If you stay in condition yellow it's unlikely that anyone will enter your personal space without you being aware of it.

In the next chapter, we will examine how to combine mental alertness with physical presence to decrease the odds of being perceived as a victim. By making simple changes in your physiology you can transform your appearance from weak to being seen as another predator.

UNDERSTANDING NON VERBAL CUES

As much as 90 percent of face to face communication is nonverbal. What is said is all too frequently not what we respond to, but rather the physical presence of the other person, their expressions, and gestures (TRS, 2011).

A lot of information is conveyed very quickly based on this information. For our average daily contact it tells us if the other person agrees with us or seems trustworthy. We make snap judgments based on this information every day. Criminals do the same thing, but they are looking for different cues. These are cues that indicate weakness, no different than a cheetah attempting to pick out the weakest of the herd on the Serengeti.

Knowing this gives us certain advantages. By projecting a certain physical image we can transform our appearance from prey to being another predator. We can also benefit by perceiving a threat by these cues before it escalates and either attempt to defuse the situation or make a tactical retreat (aka: run).

We'll start by looking at physical presence. Years ago, Oprah Winfrey did an episode that followed a White male and a Black male test subject as they looked at how people responded differently to them when they asked similar questions in the same location. The results seemed to imply that people were more likely to help and interact with the White test subject in comparison to his Black counterpart.

It was presented as a race issue. But is that accurate? Both were in similar environments asking similar questions. However, the White male was wearing preppy clothing and the Black male was wearing ghetto clothing. Do you see instantly how that conveys different information to you quite separate from race? What if the clothing were reversed? Would you feel more comfortable with a White male dressed in ghetto gear than a Black male wearing a suit?

We make immediate judgments based on such things as posture and clothing. It's not prejudice that determines your thoughts it's a natural safety instinct. It may not always be right, but whatever stereotype you are reacting to exists because there is some element of truth to it. The baggy pants held up by one hand and no belt that defines the dress code of inner city youth is based on the one-size-fits-all pants issued in jail. The image caught on with a whole generation as it immediately implied you had done your time. The kids that first adopted this look wanted to project an image of toughness. The image has now become largely cultural with few knowing how it first developed.

As you make a snap judgment based on their appearance, they are making one about you. In policing the image you project is called Command Presence. The sight of a crisp uniform and good posture is the elements that control nearly 97% of police interactions with the public. No additional force needs to be used, merely the officer's presence.

That being said, if an officer showed up on the scene of an incident with his shirt untucked, gravy stains on his tie, and his beer belly leading the way through the door, is he more likely to be challenged than someone with military bearing in exactly the same circumstance? Uniforms can only do so much.

The thing that separates the 3% that challenge the police from the 97% that don't is one simple thing. The 3% think they can win. They size up the cop and either determines immediately if they can out run or out fight the cop. They are not worried about other officers, K9s, or helicopters that can be brought to bear. The 3% are sizing up the immediate situation and weighing their odds. The sharper, fitter, and alert the officer appears the less chance he will be challenged.

The objective we all have is to present Command Presence in our daily life. Lacking the obvious benefit of a police uniform, which implies authority, we should seek out clothes that give a similar impression. In general, you'll find darker colors like black and navy blue is a better color to wear. This is similar to the idea of the power suit. A dark blue suit, white shirt, and red tie that has long been regarded as the suit for executives and businessmen because it gives a sense of dominance compared to lighter colors. Compare the power suit image to someone in a pastel leisure suit and you immediately get the sense of who is more likely to be in charge. That may or may not be true, but it is the first impression you get.

Certainly not all situations call for a suit, but the idea is to look for darker colors and attempt to dress one step up from your environment. If everyone else is in T-shirts then you should consider a polo shirt. You are not doing anything to stand out, just trying to give the impression of being slightly more prepared.

Better dress also tends to decrease the use of violence. Studies on violence in bars consistently find that dress codes significantly decreased fights among patrons. Where a bump would lead to a shove and then a punch if two people were wearing T-shirts, clubs that required better dress didn't see little bumps on a dance floor leading to fights (Berkley, 1997). Nicer clothing implies there's an expectation of better behavior and people tend to abide by that expectation.

Most people want to be judged for who they are on the inside. However, the way people make that decision is based on the image you project on the outside. Hunched shoulders and eyes peering at the ground instantly convey that you are not very confident on the inside. To a predator that means you don't pose much of a threat, making you tempting prey.

If you stand with your shoulders back, head up, and eyes moving slowly from side to side shows both confidence and alertness in an instant to a criminal. If a criminal sees this confident person and someone with slumped shoulders, staring down at the pavement walking down the same block, whom will he instantly target? Most likely, neither will be hit. The presence of someone who is confident and alert will make the other person less vulnerable. A predator sizing up his opportunity with the easy target sees the alert person as a threat he can't account for as he's attempting a crime.

Hopefully you're starting to see the benefit of taking such things as dress and posture seriously. They don't just benefit you, but offer a diffusion of benefits to others. **By simply appearing confident and alert, in the crime triangle of an offender, victim, and a location you have become a capable guardian of that location for the time that you are there. A capable guardian over a location makes crime move elsewhere. Simply take the confident, alert person out of the equation and you have all the necessary ingredients for a crime to occur.**

The objective is to stand straight but relaxed. If you stand too erect, with arms stiff at you sides and neck ramrod straight, you are presenting a look of fear. Confident people are relaxed but alert. Think of kids answering questions in class. A confident kid will shoot their hand up. A kid with very little confidence in his answer will attempt to shrink away, knees together, head down, hoping to not make eye contact. If he raises his hand it won't go much above his head, his elbow left on the desk. From the teacher's perspective, she already knows who knows the answer without hearing anything.

To project more of this confidence, feel comfortable taking up space. Like the nervous student, nervous people try to shrink away and avoid eye contact. Criminals know their answer to who will fight back just as quickly as a teacher can gauge a classroom. It's estimated that life coarse persistent criminals will commit a hundred crimes for each one that they get arrested for. They get very good at reading situations and people to determine their risks.

When gauging risk, criminals are far less likely to commit a crime if the risk is imminent. What that means is that if the odds of being beaten up or caught are high they are unlikely to commit a crime. If they may go to jail tonight they may weigh their chances. The idea that they might go to prison six months from now or even face the death penalty 10 years down the road simply doesn't register with them. Most street criminals, unlike white-collar criminals, do not have long-range expectations or goals. They don't save money, because someone else will take it. They live for short-term goals and can only perceive short-term risk. So, like the cop facing one of those 3% of people that think they can win, you have to project an image of short-term risk.

To do this, imagine two people standing in front of you. You can place them in any circumstance. They could be giving a speech, or simply standing on a corner on a dark street. One has his hands on his hips in a classic Superman pose. The other has his left arm hanging to his side, with this right arm crossed over his chest, his hand grasping his elbow. The first is claiming his space, immediately conveying that he is comfortable in this environment. The other is revealing his discomfort by attempting to shield himself behind his arms. You instinctively perceive this discomfort. A predator depends on it. It is how they pick out their prey.

Be aware of the unconscious behaviors you do that pop up every time you are uncomfortable. In such situations take a deep breath, stand tall, hands on your hips like Superman. Your physiology not only conveys how you are feeling, but by deliberately changing your physiology you can change your mindset. This doesn't just apply to self-defense situations, but it works in all occasions. When you stand relaxed and confident people immediately sense it. More importantly, it triggers the same response in you. It doesn't matter that you are neither relaxed nor confident.

The act of claiming your space is quite powerful. A study conducted by Dr. Amy Cuddy of Harvard Business, found that taking on a strong, open pose for only two minutes could increase testosterone levels by 20%, while decreasing cortisol, the stress hormone by an equal 20%. Taking a closed or protective pose has exactly the opposite effect. That is a 40% swing in positive and negative hormones simply by the pose you take. Knowing this and applying it to your daily activity can have a dynamic impact on the rest of your life. **By adopting a Superman pose throughout the day not only gives the perception of power to others, it also causes it to occur within you. A power pose can increase pain tolerance, risk taking, and willingness to take action.** In stress situations, whether it's a test, a job interview, or a potential threat, taking on a power pose not only affects the way others perceive you, it also allows you to access your very best abilities in that situation.

You can also convey confidence through eye contact. Your eyes are the principle means of revealing submissiveness or aggression and we are all too often unaware that we are doing it. An unwillingness to make eye contact reveals submissiveness. To a predator it gives two important cues. First, this person will not fight back. Second, this person won't be able to identify me after an attack. Undercover officers that act as decoys have to develop this skill set in order to be mugged. It goes completely against the nature of police patrol work that involves constantly scanning sidewalks and the horizon for anything out of the ordinary.

On the other hand, you can also lock eyes for too long. Those with aggressive personalities will perceive this as a challenge, whether it was meant that way or not. If the gaze is held for a hair too long with a slight squint you can find yourself inadvertently spurring on a fight.

The goal is to make eye contact just long enough for a head nod, to acknowledge the other person. It's the briefest of moments, but it conveys to a predator that you know he's there, you can identify him, and that you're not likely to be caught by surprise. To break eye contact you merely turn your head to continue to scan your surroundings. **If you make eye contact, but then look down, you are again displaying submissive signals.** For some readers this will be rather uncomfortable because you have naturally behaved in certain ways for years or decades. At this point, merely become aware of your natural tendencies and work at improving the signals that you give out in everyday social situations. These are learned skills that have to be practiced. It won't happen overnight and you may find yourself slipping at times. Just be aware of the subtle actions you make because those watching you are.

To see how these signals play out, imagine you are trying to take money out of an ATM. You already have a sense of apprehension. Most people estimate that the average transaction at an ATM last a minute and a half. In fact, most transactions take half that time. But because of the potential threat people sense that it is taking too long to complete the transaction and be able to move to a safer environment. In such a situation people either tend to display signs of nervousness or are oblivious to their surroundings as they attempt to rush through the transaction.

If someone walked up behind you at the ATM would you attempt to shield the keypad, or be so caught up in the process that you don't recognize that anyone is behind you? Compare that to if you are aware of the other person, turn momentarily and make eye contact, nod to acknowledge them, and return to the task at hand. Each behavior reveals something to the other individual. Only one reveals confidence. It's that attitude that you want to present in any interaction.

Briefly raising eyebrows, smiling, and winking at someone are all indicators that we make, hoping the other person reciprocates in kind. These are fine with friends, but with strangers they are unconscious behaviors that are seeking an affirmation that the other person does not pose a threat. **If you are confident, you aren't seeking confirmation, you are already confident that they are no threat to you.** You are seeking only to make eye contact and reveal nothing else from your expression.

Another physical indicator of nervousness is bringing your hands to your face, whether to brush your fingers through your hair or to scratch your nose. The action of bringing your hands to the face is an unconscious reaction to stress. In essence, it is an attempt to hide behind something, even if it's nothing more than your hands.

You want to prevent giving such cues, but also need to be aware when others begin to make them. **If someone begins to groom himself, bringing his hands to his face, hair, or start brushing his collar he is likely to be preparing for an attack. He is instinctively bringing his hands up to fight without taking a fighting stance.** If he is wearing long sleeves he may very well begin to push them up, as if preparing for the work at hand. Younger or less refined young men will keep their arms at their sides, but send all their stress into clinching their fists. If they don't clench their fists, you may see nervous shaking in the hands as blood starts to flood out of the hands to the major muscles in reaction to stress. The jaw may clinch and eyebrows furrow. An aggressor may break eye contact to focus on a target on you, or briefly look away, to draw your attention towards what he is looking at and away from an attack. Any of these subtle clues are indicators that he is only moments from taking a swing. Again, by being in condition yellow you can perceive a person's little tells and address them before they take action.

The way to control that moment is to call him on it. Most likely he doesn't even realize he is throwing off such cues. Simply ask, "Why are you tensing up?"

If you can, you want to pose a question to his behavior. You pose a question, because the person asking questions is typically the person in control. Teachers, professors, the police, game show hosts all ask questions. Instinctively, the person asking the question is perceived as being in charge. By asking a question, you are demanding an answer.

If someone questions you with such phrases as, "What are you looking at? Who do you think you are?" Simply reply with a simple question of your own, "Why do you ask?" It's completely non-confrontational, but puts you back in the position of asking the questions and doesn't show submissiveness.

In the end, the point to recognize is that each of us is constantly sizing up others based on dress, posture and eye contact. Violent street people are more in tune with these behaviors as they use them as the bread and butter of determining who will make for an easy mark.

Criminals will also physically reveal their intentions before an assault. Remain alert and challenge them at a distance to increase you chance to diffuse the situation before it becomes physical. Criminals make these unconscious actions because we all act similarly under stress. In the next chapter we will look at the natural reactions that occur in the body under stress. This understanding will help you realize that if you feel weak kneed in a violent encounter it's not because you are a coward. It's because you're human.

PHYSIOLOGICAL REACTIONS TO STRESS

Courage is being scared to death, but saddling up anyway. - John Wayne

The office is eerily quiet as you shut off the last of the lights to head home. The meeting ran an hour past what you had expected and all that was agreed upon was to schedule another meeting. The act of flipping off the lights was the only thing that gives you even a sense of satisfaction from the entire day.

You pull the door behind you and hear it make a solid click, letting you know it is locked and that the worst of the day is behind you. The parking lot is dark, aside from a few scattered street lamps throwing down circles of light throughout the night. Your car's parked at the far end of the lot. The closer spots left for customers that have long since left. As you make your way to your vehicle you hear the unmistakable sound of running footsteps comes up from your rear.

Beads of sweat immediately break out on your forehead. You can feel your hands grow cold as blood flows out of your fingers and begins to pound in your eardrums. For a moment you stiffen up, confronted with two opposing options; make a mad dash to the car, with little hope of fumbling for the keys and opening the lock, or turning and confronting the threat, knowing that it's most likely a figment of your imagination.

Suddenly, some primal instinct kicks in that drives you towards your car, but with each step, the car almost seems to be two steps further away. You regret thinking to yourself that you can make it home without stopping by the bathroom as your bladder begins to let go. The footsteps are now deafening in your ears and as you fumble for your keys, watching the twitching in your hands as if Parkinson's disease has suddenly claimed your central nervous system.

We'll freeze frame the moment as it's hardly the heroic reaction you would want in a sudden confrontation. In the previous chapter we discussed how to make your physical presence appear as both confident and aware to prevent an attack. Although alertness and physical presence are your first steps to making yourself a hard target some criminals can be desperate that they choose you as a victim.

Presenting yourself as strong, self-controlled, and confident is an image to put forth to prevent a criminal attack from occurring. But once the stress of a physical threat actually happens your basic physiology will begin to fight against you, as it will for almost 97% of people in the same situation. Even the Duke summed up courage as not confidence, but a willingness to look your own fear head on and charge towards it.

The simple fact is that the body naturally reacts to stress in a consistent pattern across people. No one likes to discuss these reactions; for fear that doing so will make him look weak. However, as soon as someone confides their fears to someone else in the same or a similar situation, the other person will invariably say, "Me too."

So, the purpose of this chapter is to cover some of the basic reactions in the body when under stress. These reactions are normal and should not be seen as embarrassing, but rather normal physiological reactions to stress. Understanding that this will happen allows you to function effectively, knowing that it isn't weakness you're experiencing, but simple hormonal effects on the body. Once you understand these reactions, we will look at ways of overcoming these physiological issues to improve performance in a physical confrontation.

The majority of this chapter is built on the work of Lt. Col. David Grossman who wrote the books 'On Combat' and 'On Killing', two of the quintessential books on the subject. He also speaks nationwide on the topic of the Bulletproof Mind. Also a tip of the hat goes to Debbie Gardner of the Survival Institute who teaches on the natural reactions of the body under stress. Any opportunity you have to read or see either Lt. Col. Grossman or Debbie Gardner should be taken.

Virtually all humans have a common set of phobias. These include the fear of snakes, falling, public speaking, and human aggression. Each of these fears create similar reactions in the body:

a. Trembling
b. Sweating
c. Chills
d. Nausea
e. Hyperventilation
f. Dizziness
g. Thirstiness
h. Urge to urinate
i. Diarrhea
j. Upset stomach
k. Jumpiness

You may experience one or more of the conditions based on a number of circumstances. But the reason these reactions occur is because of a natural reaction to stress called vasoconstriction. Under stress your body constricts blood to the inner parts of the body in an attempt to protect you from injuries to the extremities, while flooding the bigger muscle groups with more energy. As blood flows from the extremities the body is able to suffer minor wounds to the skin and to the arms and legs that will cause very little bleeding. However, this lack of blood will cause a loss of fine motor skills particularly in the hands and fingers. When you have spoken in public and felt your throat get dry, the vocal cords constrict, and watched the notes in your hand shaking vigorously as you turned ghostly white it's because your body is undergoing vasoconstriction.

This same process leads to auditory exclusion where sounds are completely or largely blocked out. At the same time tunnel vision kicks in, eliminating all vision on your periphery, allowing you to only focus directly on what's ahead. Both reactions have benefits of causing your mind to pick out a specific target, but they become detrimental when you are facing multiple attackers.

If too many things come at you too fast your body will go into sensory overload. If a loud noise, combined with blinding light are mixed with the pound of a shockwave a person can simply shut down as all the senses become overwhelmed. This is the premise behind flash bang grenades, not to harm people, but to overwhelm their system, preventing them from attacking. Being that a battlefield is a nonstop combination of all of these elements, it becomes clear how soldiers go into shell shock or Post-traumatic stress disorder (PTSD).

After you undergo a high stress situation your para-sympathetic nervous system takes over, essentially throwing your body into a state of utter fatigue. The purpose is to shut your body off so that you can recover from whatever it was that you dealt with. Pain that may have been blotted out of you mind during the incident will now suddenly become readily apparent. Those who suffer from PTSD are largely locked into this state, having difficulty returning to normal function.

This entire process is the normal reaction of your body under stress. It is nothing to be embarrassed about. It is normal. However, there are steps you can take to overcome these natural effects and help you react in a more effective manner.

TRAINING

The primary way to battle these effects is to be put into controlled high stress situations. Learning to deal with stressful conditions develops a knowledge base that builds confidence that you can deal with other high stress conditions. Being placed in stressful situations simply makes the next event, or that one critical event, easier to handle. Compare a headlining standup comic to an open mic comic. The open mic comic doesn't have years of working smoky rooms, watching other comics, and dealing with hecklers to fall back on as he takes to the stage. The headliner takes to the stage with a confidence built on the knowledge that he has failed before and it didn't kill him. He is certain that whatever this crowd may do he has seen before and he can trust his material to make them laugh. An open mic comic has no such confidence.

This allows for an autopilot response. Through repetition your body will react naturally to whatever is before it. If you train consistently with a handgun to put the front sight on center mass and apply a smooth trigger press, under stress your mind will simply say "front sight and smooth trigger press," while your body simply repeats what it has practiced.

In a similar manner, if someone attacks while your hands are empty, if you have consistently practiced striking to the throat, it will not matter what your attacker is doing or what direction he comes. You will react automatically and he will be reacting to you and most likely losing consciousness.

Under stress you never rise to the occasion, you will regress to the level of your training, locked into very basic fundamentals. You can imagine being attacked by a stranger and having no practice or plan. What would you do? Lock up, not certain of what to do? Flail at your attacker, just hoping that something lands and stops him?

Compare that to someone that has at least put it in their mind that if I'm attacked I will strike as hard as I can into his neck, knowing that I will either shut off blood to the brain, or air to the body. If the first blow doesn't work, I'm going to continue until I shut him down. This is a simple, basic plan using simple, basic technique. By practicing simple techniques you will unconsciously react to a physical confrontation through muscle memory.

In a physical confrontation you will be scared. This fear will naturally cause certain physiological changes in your body that will make you think that only a coward would feel this way. But that is fiction. You are merely experiencing a natural reaction to stress. **It is a rare individual that has nerves of steel. The people that survive are the ones that learn to steel their nerves.** As WWI fighting ace, Eddie Rickenbacker, put it "Courage is doing what you are afraid to do. There can be no courage unless you are scared." This statement is from the guy acknowledged as the greatest WW1 fighter pilot and who once took on 7 German planes in a single battle.

The physiological and psychological stress that hits you under combat is likely to cause you to only perform half as well as you do in training. To increase the effectiveness of your training you need to practice under stress. For someone considering defending him or herself with a gun, this can be done by running 100 yards, dropping to do ten push-ups and then engaging a target, or practicing dry firing with a handgun. Such physical stress is not exactly like hormonal stress, but it does increase your heart rate and cause blood to flow to major, core muscles rather than to your extremities.

To push your stress levels up on both your body and mind you can compete head to head with someone else in a tactical course or a steel plate challenge. You can combine this sort of competition with an additional challenge of putting your hands into ice, to mimic the loss of fine motor skills under stress. Firing a pistol quickly and accurately after allowing your hands to lose their feeling takes the level of difficulty up dramatically.

When you compete head to head it helps you understand that in a physical confrontation you and your opponent will both experience the same physiological reactions. In real life, if he is only prepared to intimidate you, or immediately gain compliance through fear, he is unlikely to be prepared for an aggressive reaction from you. Now, suddenly, all of the same hormonal reactions will begin to happen in his body. If his plan to overwhelm you changes, he will only have running as a viable alternative.

Lock in your mind that you will continue to shoot, strike, and react whether you are stabbed, shot, or wet yourself. If you expect to get out of a fight without a scrape then you have unrealistic expectations.

You also have to develop a mindset that you are willing to cause injury to someone attacking you. One of the most intriguing findings that Lt. Col. Grossman identified is that humans instinctively are unwilling to kill other humans. We are not designed that way. It is the rare individual that is classified as a sociopath or a psychopath that holds no remorse in harming others. Thankfully, this only applies to about 3% of the population.

Because of this basic instinct to not kill other humans, during WWI only about 10% of soldiers would actively fire at the enemy. By Vietnam that number had increased to nearly 90%. The dramatic difference was due to a change in training. Where WWI soldiers trained at bull's-eye shooting, by Vietnam the targets had changed to head and shoulders human silhouettes. Often these would flash in front of the soldier, causing him to react to the shape and movement. This meant that a soldier didn't pause to consider that he was shooting at another human being, but merely reacting to an image that appeared aggressive.

This reveals the importance of having some training where you begin to react instinctively, rather than overly analyzing your actions. Such a delay only costs you time and potentially your life. Unfortunately, many of the active shooters that we've seen over the past two decades have unconsciously practiced these very same drills as they numbed themselves to violence through first shooter video games. When they finally decide to go on a real life killing rampage, they are largely reacting no differently than they do during endless hours of shooting at a digital enemy in cyberspace. This is similar to the radicalism of Islamic militants. They are taught a religious hatred and given a justification for killing. By being so engrossed in demeaning other religions and nationalities they are able to view their actions as not killing another human being, but destroying something evil in the name of Allah.

Police and military train in a similar way to first shooter video games by being placed in front of a video screen (FATS) and having to react in either a shoot or don't shoot scenario. This type of training causes officers to confront situations that they will likely face in the street and make instinctive reactions if the actor in the video suddenly goes for a gun, or a badge. This type of shoot-don't-shoot training challenges you to react quickly, but also make good moral decisions at the same time. Most first person shooter games have no such requirement, only accuracy and body counts.

Police also train in force on force skills by use of simunitions. Using modified versions of real handguns officers are put into a confrontation with suspect(s) armed with similar pistols or rifles firing paint rounds. As you can imagine, this type of training is far more realistic and stressful than standing on a firing line and shooting holes in a paper target at the sound of a whistle.

From a practical aspect, you can mimic this type of training using first person shooting games that involve shoot/don't shoot scenarios and through paintball competition. Both allow you the ability to practice reactive shooting, however, paintball will place you under far greater stress, as there is likely pain associated with being hit. If you train to continue to fight despite being hit, you develop a mindset to fight through injury. If you give up after you are shot, you will likely train yourself to give up in real combat.

In a similar way, you should practice unarmed fighting with someone in some form of controlled training. If you have practiced a martial art that is big on katas and techniques for belt ranking you have developed a skill set without practical experience. You need to train with a partner so that you are not shocked when you get struck in the nose and realize how little force is really required to cause pain to certain areas of the body.

Whether training with a weapon or empty handed, your goal is to act through muscle memory, where the skills are so engrained that you do them instinctively. You don't want or need to learn hundreds of possible skills. You need only a handful that you can do naturally without thought. As an example, there are multiple ways to clear a malfunction in a semi auto pistol. However, tapping the magazine with the palm of your hand and racking the slide will clear virtually all jams. Why train differently to clear different malfunctions when it's easier and faster to react the same way to all jams so you don't waste time figuring out what happened?

Hick's law states that the more options you have, the slower the reaction time. You can well understand why this becomes important when under the stress of an attack. The more things you have to think about with a handgun or the more places you attempt to hit an opponent the more time you waste. If you have a simple handgun and focus on some fundamental skills you will react quicker than with a complex gun and unnecessary movement. Unarmed, if you train to strike essentially one target, that is equally effective no matter a person's size, you immediately eliminating any possible delay in reaction.

One final thought on training is that it is simply the preparation for the possible. The more you train the more instinctive your reaction will become. In truth, what this allows you to do is act rather than react in any given circumstance. You know immediately what you will do in a critical event instead of wondering what to do. Even if your training is nothing more than mentally preparing yourself for the possibility of an attack and recognizing that you are allowed to defend yourself and to do so aggressively sets the stage for you to win in a physical encounter

BREATHING

Even with proper training, when you are under stress your body will do a number of things that can negatively affect your ability to act confidently. Fear causes a common reaction in virtually everyone. If you are walking down a hallway and someone jumped out and yelled, "Boo!" what is you natural reaction? You immediately jerk back, take in a deep breath and hold it. You hold your breath until you realize that there is no real threat. Once you know it's a prank, you let out a sigh of relief or laugh in recognition that you've been spooked.

But what if it is a real threat? You walk between several cars and suddenly someone jumps out and tries to grab you. You take in a deep breath and freeze. Rather than experiencing a sudden breath out in relief you lock up. Breathing that happens naturally every moment of everyday simply stops. By holding your breath, the brain and body become starved for oxygen, limiting your ability to fuel muscles for action and your mind from developing a plan.

You have to shake yourself from this natural reaction. The shout associated with martial arts is an attempt to overcome this reaction. In order to shout, you have to forcibly breathe out, breaking your body from holding its breath. The breath should come out as a growl.

When you are under stress, your neck naturally contracts, making screaming difficult, if not impossible to do. A growl is far easier to accomplish and is the natural way athletes exhale when exerting themselves. Think of the sound a weight lifter makes struggling for a single rep max or a tennis player makes during a serve. This growl is guttural, animalistic and the last thing a criminal wants to hear from a victim.

Taking in a deep breath in surprise and then letting it out is no different than the deep breath you frequently see just before someone gives a speech. By taking a deep breath you regain composure, flood your body with oxygen, and regain your ability to reason and react.

GRIP

When under stress your heart begins pounding so hard you can feel the pulse in your ears and swear you could see your heart beating under your clothes. Despite the increase in heart rate, less blood is reaching your extremities. Arteries narrow to the hands and feet as blood rushes away from the skin. Blood floods the major muscles and your core, causing your fingers to quiver violently. This can be seen clearly in anyone holding papers when talking in public while holding their notes. The pages look like a nonexistent breeze is blowing them around.

To get blood back to your hands, clinch your hands into fists or grip something tightly. This simple action helps bring blood back to your extremities and allows you to perform better at fine motor skills. When something startling happens when you are gripping something, you will naturally grip it harder. This is most clearly seen when driving. If someone veers into your lane, suddenly both hands grip the wheel until your knuckles turn white. However, without something in your hands, you lose this natural reaction. This shows that beyond the mechanical advantage provided by a weapon, the mere clinching of it helps overcome the nervousness of a stressful event.

Real life and death violence puts your body into an immediate state of intense fear, causing blood to leave the hands and feet, and flood the major muscle groups in a means of fueling fight or flight. With a loss of fine motor skill your ability to use a clever wrist technique or a come-along hold that took months to master goes straight out the window. What will work is a sudden surge of adrenaline to your core and major muscles, making big, directed strikes more powerful. If you can focus the strikes you can become very effective at defending yourself by injuring him.

Along with the immediate physical reactions of fight and flight that kick in, there are psychological issues that also need to be addressed. A violent attack can cause a multitude of negative thoughts to kick in at exactly the wrong time. They are thoughts that cause you to question why you are there and if you can survive the situation.

To overcome this, it's common practice in law enforcement to keep a picture of your family in your hat or on your clipboard to remind yourself that you need to return home to those you love. It gives you something more to live for than yourself, recognizing that if you don't survive it's not just you that are being harmed. If you are killed your wife and kids are left on their own.

This recognition is powerful. If you think, I couldn't fight off someone with an axe attacking me. What if someone with an axe were attacking your kids? Could you muster up the ability to defend them? In fact, you are more than likely quite confident that you would kill anyone that attacked your kids.

Making this change in your thinking is the light switch you need to click to win a violent encounter. It gives you the confidence to fight back that you might lack if defending yourself alone. Seeing someone attack a loved one creates a righteous indignation that drives you to act and act aggressively. You know immediately and without question that what is happening is wrong. However, when we are attacked we tend to blame ourselves. All sorts of negative thoughts immediately strike us: Am I over reacting? I knew I shouldn't have come here. He's bigger. If I fight back he'll only hurt me more.

To escape this negative thinking, you need to think in terms of serving something larger than yourself when attacked. Not only will your family be devastated if you are killed, but you have to think what if this person goes on to rape or kill someone else? It's your opportunity and responsibility to stop his actions now.

The first part of this book covered the real truth of crime. It tends to be highly localized to both certain people and locations. This knowledge gives you an advantage to substantially decrease your likelihood of victimization. However, life is not without risk. Crime can occur anywhere that an opportunity exists. More kids are becoming increasingly isolated, filling the void in their life with first person shooter games. Some decide to make such games into real life events. The diaries of many of these kids show they study others that have gone on similar killing sprees. They record how and what their predecessors did, and what the body count was. Their objective is to get a higher score. At the same time, others are becoming radicalized in militant Islam. In either case, they are dehumanizing other people and simply see them as a means to an end. Active shooters and terrorists both target areas where the largest body count is possible. Unless you choose to be a hermit, the demands of work and leisure may very well put you into locations that increase your odds of being a target.

That doesn't make you wrong for being there. You should not feel guilty for being a good person in bad circumstance, or allow others to make you feel that way. Victims don't create the circumstance; the criminal does. You simply need to learn to handle the circumstance. You do that by changing your way of thinking. **An attack against you is an attack against those you love.** This gives you the capacity to act aggressively to defend others and a willingness to do anything to survive. This gives you courage. **Courage isn't the absence of fear, but the willingness to stare it down.** This is a combat mindset. This is a mindset to survive.

As we covered earlier, the Crime Triangle requires an offender, victim, and a place. Take away any of those and a crime can't occur. We also know that an outside force controls each side of the Crime Triangle. An offender has a handler, which could be a parent, spouse, or probation officer. A place has a manager, which is often the owner of a location. And a victim has a GUARDIAN. This can be the police, security, or it can be YOU. If you view yourself as a guardian you have taken the victim out of the equation. When you take on the responsibility to defend whoever is in a location, even if it is only you, then crime is being attacked the moment you enter the space.

Unarmed Survival

A good plan, violently executed now, is better than a perfect plan next week. - Patton

The foundation of this book is built around the idea of directly affecting the two sides of the Crime Triangle that you have the ability to control. You have the ability to make your home, business, car, or personal property less tempting by taking exactly the same steps you would take to make yourself less of a victim. This is accomplished through using the techniques of Situational Crime Prevention defined by Ronald Clarke as increasing a criminal's effort, increasing his immediate risks, reducing his rewards, not provoking his attention, and removing any excuse he may have to target you or your property. In essence, you are target hardening both yourself and your property. This is accomplished by such things as strengthening doorjambs, posting signs, and defining your space, to standing straight and remaining aware of your surroundings.

By following the ideas presented above you are accomplishing the primary means of eliminating crime - Avoidance. This should be the bedrock of your crime prevention plan. However, the best laid plans of mice and men often go awry. To that end, the following chapters are designed to give you the skill set to defend yourself if a situation goes from bad to worse.

The earlier part of the book focused on being in condition yellow to prevent a crime. Now we are moving into condition red where you are actively engaged in a physical fight. To help define when you go to condition red it is good to look at a concept that Colonel Jeff Cooper developed to virtually eliminate all accidental causes of injury by a firearm. These concepts are simple, but to this day these four tenants are reinforced in every firearms training environment.

Treat all guns as if they are loaded.
Never let the muzzle cover anything you are not willing to destroy.
Keep your finger off the trigger until your sights are on the target.
Be sure of your target and what is beyond it.

With a tip of the hat to Colonel Cooper's four tenants of firearms safety, with slight modifications they can be adapted to any use of force.

Assume in every situation that the opponent is armed.
Never use violence unless you intend to destroy that person.
Keep your hands, feet, knees, and elbows to yourself until you have to react.
Be aware of your surroundings. If there is one threat, there are likely to be others.

These four concepts really change the way that you look at all "unarmed" defense.

•Assume in every situation that the opponent is armed:

If you treat any physical encounter as a match with a referee, you lose. If you are attacked or threatened he has intent to harm you. You have no idea what he is willing to do to accomplish his mission, or what he has brought with him to help win the fight. If you get the upper hand in a grappling match and he senses that he is going to lose, will he use a knife to gain an advantage? Don't take the risk. If you're wrong, you could die.

68

•Never use violence unless you intend to destroy that person.

If you are armed with a gun and you pull the trigger, you have made a split second decision that an aggressor's actions are so threatening that you are willing to kill him to save your own life or the life of someone else. There is no other time or reason to fire a gun at someone. The same applies to fighting without a gun. If you are forced to use violence, you better intend to destroy your opponent as quickly as possible. There is no need for flashy kicks or clever techniques. You must simple act quickly and decisively with the intent to cause an injury that will immediately stop his aggression. You stop when there is no longer a threat.

•Keep your hands, feet, knees, and elbows to yourself until you have to react.

You are not spoiling for a fight. This is not a typical Tuesday night at an Irish pub. This is not fighting for ego, sport, or a title belt. You are not out posturing and wanting to take on all comers. This is a situation where you ended up at 1 am getting out late from work, tired from a 16-hour day, wanting to be in bed asleep and trying to figure out how many hours of sleep you can get before you have to do it all over again. As you pull your keys out for your car someone sees you as a preoccupied, viable target. After all, you've worked all day. You probably have something of value from all your hard work. In such a situation, what is he willing to do to get what he wants? You have no idea. Don't limit your response. React decisively; doing only what is necessary to stop the immediate threat.

•Be aware of your surroundings: If there is one threat, there are likely to be others.

Criminals make rational decisions, even if the decisions are rational only to the criminal himself. As we covered earlier, this is called Rational Choice Theory (Clarke and Cornish, 1985) and it makes it clear that it's rare that criminals act completely irrationally. They may act on the spur of the moment, but oftentimes they will have planned out a criminal attack. In doing so, they want to make sure they get away safe. That means a robber will either use an accomplice to help overwhelm a victim, or will be spurred on by the peer pressure of the group he is with. Don't think you are safe because you took out an immediate threat. Be aware of your surroundings. There might be others.

Keep these basic four ideas towards the use of violence in mind:

Assume in every situation that the opponent is armed.
Never use violence unless you intend to destroy that person.
Keep your hands, feet, knees, and elbows to yourself until you have to react.
Be aware of your surroundings. If there is one threat, there are likely to be others.

With this basic understanding you see that your objective is to avoid violence at all cost, but aware that when it's necessary to use force it must be aggressive. These ideas work because normal people don't attack you. The vast majority of people that you interact with have been properly socialized that violence is wrong. Only those that have not been socialized properly rely on violence, because they lack the social skills to get what they want through normal interactions. It really doesn't matter if it is poor genetics or bad upbringing that led to this behavior, only that such people are driven by serving their immediate wants and desires and have almost no capacity to empathize with anyone else.

Such criminals tend to think only in the moment. Long-term planning is not part of their repertoire. If they want something, they will do what's necessary to get it. Even if it only serves their immediate needs with little regard to the consequences. Knowing this wakes you up to the reality that fighting back against such a person requires a similar lack of concern for their wellbeing. Grips, holds, and strikes to non-vital areas are unlikely to stop such an attacker. Whether it's your wallet or your life, a psychopath's focus will be to take it. Unfortunately, you don't have the luxury of knowing if it is merely money they want. **To survive you must be willing to cause sufficient harm to him so that he can't cause it to you. You need to resolve in your mind that a physical assault against you requires a deliberate response of crippling or killing your attacker; no different than if you were armed with a gun.**

If you are attacked you have very little time to determine how an attacker is armed. Would you react differently if he's got a gun, knife, or is empty handed? If you operate under the idea that he is armed and focus on taking out his ability to use any weapon by striking in and through vital areas you are more likely to survive. **You are not looking to just hit him, but hitting him with the intent to cause an immediate injury, such as striking to the side of the neck, throat, or eyes.**

Physical fights almost always go to the person that lands the first blow. The first blow disorients the opponent and the follow up strikes only cause more and more damage. This puts the other person in a defensive position. You don't win fights by blocking. You win by hitting. Real fights rarely play out like Rocky, with one fighter getting the upper hand and then the other turns the tables. Fights typically go to the person who strikes first, and certainly to the one who is able to cause a debilitating injury. The movie 'Taken' shows realistically how an aggressive first strike can end a fight. Although Liam Neeson's character often pulls off a cool wrist take down, throw, or arm lock, the technique is set up by a strike to the throat to weaken the attacker. No matter the opponent's action or size, whether grabbing or punching, a strike to the throat immediately stops the threat and leads to the end of the fight.

Most fights devolve into one side catching the other with a good blow then using the weak hand to brace the victim while the aggressor pounds away repeatedly on the face or body with the strong hand. Far from needing years of training it's simple and brutal. If you think you beat it with fancy technique, you will be pummeled.

Such a simple, aggressive action is critical in a violent encounter. When you are attacked suddenly you cannot be certain that your attacker is unarmed or operating alone. If you get caught up in grappling or going to the ground a weapon can easily trump your ground game, or an unexpected companion can strike you in the back of the head while you are tied up with his friend. You need to keep to your feet to avoid additional attacks and any potential weapons.

Because of the nature of violence it must be reserved for only life and death encounters. Any situation where you want to get even or defend your ego needs to be resolved through communication or walking away. Using violence is only for the extremely rare moments where all other options are gone. Because these moments are so extremely rare, they also require extreme uses of force to make sure you survive. **If you can't say that you feared for your life then you need to find an alternative to solving your problem than violence. Playing with any violence is the same as playing with a loaded** gun - stupid. Don't be stupid.

Violence is violence, whether you're using your bare hands or are armed with a pistol. You are intending to stop a threat and the only way to do so is by making sure your opponent cannot injure you. If you view a violent, unarmed encounter as somehow on a lesser scale of violence than an armed encounter you will limit your response. That can prove to be deadly. You can't risk finding out how far he's willing to go. You have to be willing to end it now. That simple mindset gives you the ability to prevail. Skill is secondary.

By seeing violent encounters in this way you can see that it doesn't require years of training to win. It's a mindset. A typical victim has not thought about how to react if attacked. This makes their response weak, as they are unprepared. At best these victims try to gain compliance with slaps to the face or pounding on the attacker's chest. Such measures would deter someone simply playing with you, but not someone intent on moving you somewhere else or taking your life. Instead, simply flip that switch in your mind that gives you permission to focus on basics strikes to critical areas of his body to stop his attack. You have to continue striking in the same area until the opponent is no longer a threat.

Even if you're armed, it's likely that the first action that you take will be with your empty hands. Most law enforcement officers operate under the macho driven, but naive idea that if this or that happens they'll simply go for their gun. That is certainly a primary drill trained by most agencies to build reaction speed and muscle memory. However, the FBI conducted drills to show that a knife-wielding attacker can close a distance of 21 feet and strike an officer with a gun in an open carry holster before he can draw. It is important to recognize that even if you are armed in order to get to your weapon you may first have to react by moving or doing an unarmed defensive action against an aggressive attacker.

To win a violent encounter means that biting, screaming, and gouging, all the things that mom told you not to do as a kid, should be your objective. However, **the most effective strike is a strike with the edge of the hand to the throat. No matter an attacker's size, a strike to the throat causes the offender to fight for air. His arms will naturally react by defensively clutching at the throat, making any additional attack a secondary thought.**

Even if you miss the throat and strike the side of the neck you will stun your attacker and potentially cause unconsciousness, as blood flow is temporary blocked to the brain at the carotid artery. My sensei once did a demonstration using me as the uke, which is apparently Japanese for 'stupid one.' He struck me in the side of my neck with a blow so hard that it felt like it reverberated down my entire spine, completely stunning me. He told me that he only struck me with about 25% force. I would hazard to say it was closer to 50%, but either way, it made it clear to me how devastating a blow to the neck can be.

Other targets that you can utilize are any structurally weak point on the human body. The reason to target these spots is because they are consistent across people and body sizes. It doesn't matter if the person is 5'4" or 6'4" it will cause the same immediate, debilitating reaction. Some of these targets include:

Striking to the eyes: Even a flick or scratch of the eye causes a natural flinching. However, a gouge can be devastating and immediately end an attack.

Grabbing and twisting flesh: There are throws done entirely by pain. If you can find a willing partner (he will only be willing once) slap the side of his body with both hands right at the ribs, grab the flesh on both sides and pull it tight, as if rolling it from your pinky up to your forefinger between your fists. The pain is so intense your opponent will go up on his toes. All you have to do is simply hold on and sit back. He will fly over top of you to avoid the pain.

Groin strikes can end a fight even from a glancing blow, but grabbing, twisting, and pulling can guarantee it.

The elbow is one of the hardest and smallest striking points on the body. If you are in close with an opponent where punches and chops have little power, an elbow can be devastating. The power comes from a twist at the waist and through the shoulders. A strike to the temple, neck, or nose with your elbow will stop an aggressor immediately.

It's been an age-old adage to not kick a man when he's down. I would argue there's no easier time to do it. There are certainly few more effective ways of taking a person out of a fight.

Head butting - Bruce Lee, known for his flashy techniques in cinema, was asked what technique he would use in a real fight. He simply said he'd grab his opponent around the neck and drive his head into his nose. Not flashy, but quick and effective.

There is nothing about the above that would be considered fair play. And certainly nothing complicated. However, violent encounters are not sporting events. If you want to see it in mathematical terms: **Fair play = you lose.** It's that simple. The trouble is that good people are good because they abide by social convention in virtually all situations. In most encounters you have in life this serves you well. People with good intentions and who treat others fairly are more likely to succeed in life.

Therein lies the problem in a violent encounter. **Those that rely on violence either did not socialize well, or saw it as a sign of weakness. Because of their socialization they are not successful, thus putting them in a position where violence not only solves problems, but it becomes mandatory. Violent people are by nature asocial people and will not even comprehend the concept of fair play.**

The life course criminal, adolescent limited criminal, or psychopath are not regulated by the norms of society. For adolescents and life course persistent criminals the frontal cortex has not fully developed, making their actions emotionally driven rather than logical. To expect them to play fair, pull punches, or have sympathy during an assault will not happen. They are driven to take what they want whether it's your property or your life. In the moment of an attack you don't have the benefit of knowing what lengths he will go to take either from you. Unless you are willing to respond with an equal or greater amount of force, he wins. It's that simple.

The socialization that you have learned and adopted in life has probably served you well in conventional life. However, it becomes a handicap when asocial events occur. **Socialization can be deadly when disaster occurs. It's called a 'normalcy bias', where people lack the mental state or skills necessary to deal with situations outside the norm.** When buildings catch fire, people often die inside even though all they needed to do was swing a chair against a window to break the glass and create a means of escape. They were socialized that it's wrong to break windows. They failed to realize that normal behavior is no longer beneficial and they were no longer in a conventional setting.

That's why you have to fully grasp that a violent encounter is not dealt with an increasing use of force continuum like police utilize. You are unlikely to have the resources that police have available. You will only have seconds to react. Once someone threatens, grabs, hits, or pushes you then you must react with an equal or greater amount of force. How much force is he willing to use? Unless you are blessed with clairvoyance you have no idea what level he is willing to go, so you must use sufficient force to end the battle.

Once you understand that, you have liberated your ability to win in a violent encounter. You are taking away the one thing that an asocial person has that allows them to have power over his victim; He is not afraid of hurting you. When you no longer are concerned about hurting him, you can strike hard at the throat, eyes, groin, knee and not feel regret. **His injury is a direct result of the decision that he made, not your reactions to them.**

When you understand that if he wins he could kill you, you better intend to strike the areas of the body that will simply prevent that from happening. Adopting this mindset allows you to win a fight against someone younger, stronger, or bigger than you without years of training. Their eyes, throat, knees, groins are all fair game, and not protected by the amount of muscle surrounding them. Even someone with large hands, if you grab their index finger in one hand and middle finger in the other and rip them apart as hard as you can will drop them to their knees. Such aggressive behavior can debilitate even the most aggressive opponent.

Whatever strike you use you need to think in terms of overwhelming your opponent. You are not dancing around a ring defending your ground. Instead you must strike towards a specific target and drive your body towards them, forcing the offender to begin backpedaling. This doesn't allow your attacker to look for your weakness, as he is too busy trying to get you off of him.

This immediately turns the tables on an aggressor that is not used to having to defend himself. This, quite simply, is powerful. Violence is a tool to asocial people. They rely on this tool because it frequently serves them at taking things from others that they cannot get by providing a useful skill or service to them. They are specialist in fear, violence, and intimidation. However, they are not well equipped to defend against it.

You can see that you don't need a lot of technical skill with locks, flips, or holds to defend yourself. You need only the intent to cause an injury by targeting a specific weak point on an attacker. Knowing that you must survive for your family and to prevent future attacks to others allows you to focus your attention on striking forcefully to his throat with any strike available. Whether you strike with the web of the hand between the thumb and forefinger, with the edge of the hand, or with a small flashlight, the intent is to survive the fight by causing a temporary or potentially permanent incapacitating injury.

In most circumstances, when you are striking, you are using your hand as a chopping tool, not as a punching tool. Fingers and wrists frequently suffer the brunt of a punch as much as the target. Try punching a concrete wall with a closed fist. You will naturally pull the punch, knowing that it will hurt. Try chopping at a concrete wall with the side of the hand. You'll quickly find out that you could strike it harder than you did without any ill effects.

A chop, compared to a fist, also focuses the strike on a far more specific target. A chop may even miss the throat and strike the chest first, but then slide up under the chin as you follow through. A fist, on the other hand, may very well not reach the throat, being blocked first by the chest and chin.

Unarmed defense is no different than armed defense. All that changes is the tool and the target. The intent remains the same, to use violence to end an attack by causing enough injury that your attacker cannot continue his attack. With a handgun the primary target is the chest cavity. This is the target you are most likely to hit under the stress of a violent encounter that can also stop a threat. Even then multiple shots may be necessary to cause enough damage to prevent an attack. Although a person's intent is only to stop the threat, the reality of pointing and firing a gun at another human being is the recognition that he could die from your actions. You don't have the luxury of thinking maybe I can wound him to gain compliance. If you have been forced into firing at another human it must be fueled by intent to cause harm sufficient to end any response from your aggressor. The idea of shooting an attacker in the arm or leg doesn't understand the difficulty of such a shot under stress. More importantly, it lacks understanding that there is no certainty of the threat being stopped. Multiple shots to non-vital body parts simply will not stop a drugged or motivated offender.

In a situation where you are without a gun, nothing changes. Your goal remains ending the threat, recognizing that the force you are using will cause injury, and potentially death. You have to understand that anything less will leave you as the one who is injured or dead. If you are required to use violence, then you must eliminate the threat. No matter the size of the opponent, or the weapon he may have. The quickest, most certain means of stopping the threat is to stop his ability to continue an assault by disrupting his ability to breathe.

There are several reasons why the throat should be your primary target. As it is important for you to breathe under stress it also makes logical sense to take away an opponent's ability to do the same. If you hold your breath you are limiting the oxygen that is feeding your brain's ability to think and your body's ability to react. Why not simply take that ability away from an attacker?

In addition, the throat does not require a remarkable amount of force in order to stop an attacker immediately. Debbie Gardner in her self-defense seminars reveals the amount of force necessary to strike the throat by using a paper towel tube. If you can squeeze a paper towel tube or dent it with a strike, you have the ability to cause the amount of damage necessary to stop an attack.

As we covered earlier, Hick's Law states that the more options you have, the slower your reaction time. You can well understand why this becomes important when under the stress of an attack. Even those with a martial arts background can get a brain freeze when an opponent moves differently than they expected or they mess up their technique, causing them to blank for just a moment not knowing what to do next. However, if you plan to only strike one target no matter the type of attack or the person's size you immediately eliminate any possible delay in your reaction.

In 'Indian Jones Raiders of the Lost Ark', Indy finds himself confronted by a sword wielding opponent set on hacking the hero to pieces. The script called for an epic battle pitting the sword against Indy's whip. However, Harrison Ford was suffering from the flu the day the scene was scheduled to shoot. To avoid delays in the filming, while the opponent swings the massive sword around his body, taunting Indy to fight, Indy simply shoots him.

The scene gets a laugh, because it's unexpected and goes completely against formulas expected in action adventure movies. But the scene reveals a number of points very true in a real life confrontation. First, an opponent will strike when you have the flu, or when your back is turned, or anytime they think they have the upper hand. Second, the person that wins a fight is the one that delivers the blow that ends the fight. There's no need for fancy skills. That's for film. **What is effective in ending a fight is the first one to strike with brutal efficiency.**

Few things show this more clearly than the current knock out game to see the reality of violence. The knock out game involves no touching gloves and squaring up with an opponent. It is simply walking up behind someone and trying to knock him or her out with a single blow. Who do you think tends to win such an occurrence? It's the person landing the first blow. It also reveals the importance of remaining in condition yellow, to avoid allowing the situation to develop.

That's why street thugs with no formal martial arts training can defeat black belts in real life fights. The black belt has trained to play within certain rules, to use certain techniques, and to confront an opponent in a back and forth match, trying to out skill the other fighter. A street thug simply knows what he wants and will get it using overwhelming force to take it. The only defense to such an opponent is pure aggression focused on causing injury severe enough that he is unable to accomplish his goal.

Most of us who have practiced the martial arts hope that when confronted with a real life threat we will win an epic battle like the climax of an action film. But real violence is not a squaring up of equals. **Your attacker chose you because of convenience, your inattentiveness, or a perceived weakness. To win and get what he wants he will injure you to the point that you no longer pose a threat. The only way to defeat that mindset is to shut it down with focused, intense force using the strongest areas of your body, or item at hand, against the most vulnerable points on his body. Your attack must be intensely driven to eliminate the threat by causing immediate, intense injury or unconsciousness.** It will look more like the host of nameless extras knocked out with a blow or two rather than the climatic fight scene on a cliff.

You must push out of your mind that you need years of training to win a physical confrontation. To win in sports combat requires skill and strength. **But true violence has little to do with physical size, rather it depends more on striking at specific weak points on the body, and a willingness to do so.** If the thought causes you to be squeamish that's actually a good thing. Recognizing the potential damage that can be done to you or that you can do to another makes you appreciate the importance of avoiding confrontations altogether.

Waiting for the perfect moment to attack rarely comes. Most fights occur swiftly and in limited range. The attacker will almost always have the benefit of surprise and have already defined what his intentions are. If he merely asks for money, or demands it, there is no reason not to give that up. If that is the sole intention, it is scarcely worth a struggle.

However, if he is physically attacking or wants to move you to a different location, you need to respond immediately and aggressively. Any attempt to move you elsewhere will only put the attacker at an additional advantage. Moving a victim from the current location makes it clear the attacker doesn't feel completely comfortable in the immediate environment. There are too many potential guardians that could appear unexpectedly. If you are moved elsewhere, all advantages go to him. He will take you to a location which he alone controls.

Although you can't wait for a perfect moment, there are times that his ability to react to your first action will be delayed. The first is while he is talking. As he is talking he's processing his words, not focused on the assault itself. If you react during that moment, your actions will likely defeat his reactions.

You can have similar advantage if you respond affirmatively to something he says. If he demands you move, say, "alright, alright, whatever you say," and begin to follow his command. This compliance puts him at ease and allows you to begin movement. After all, not only is he expecting movement, he is demanding it. You agree to what he is saying while aggressive moving towards a specific, fight-ending target.

To go to this level of response is not something intended for a bar fight where an argument over football leads to punches being thrown. Such situations escalate due to ego and are easily diffused by avoiding the situation, agreeing with the person, or a simple tactical retreat. This type of event is a situation where you have tried to avoid a high-risk environment, but suddenly found yourself confronted by someone physically attacking you.

Most confrontations can be solved by avoidance or communication skills, even if it entails turning tail and allowing the aggressor to 'win' an argument. A violent encounter on the other hand is deadly serious and has to be stopped immediately. At these times a severe, violent response is the only answer. His intention is to shut you down. If you approach the situation with anything less than a clear objective of shutting him down first, he will win. Trying to control him, or block his strikes puts you in a losing battle. You need to have him attempting to block your attack while you simply overwhelm him and move on.

Fighting fair is a losing proposition. Striking the throat, side of the neck, thumbs in the eyes, a kick through the knee are the actions that win street fights. You are not trying to win a competition, but leave the scene under your own power. While sporting combat prepares you to fight with rules, you must learn to fight by violating the rules. Anything that is considered a violation in the ring should be what you go to first in street survival. Some call it fighting dirty. In reality, it's fighting, plain and simple. You may like to think that you are above it, but a criminal will depend on it. If you aren't playing by no rules, you'll lose.

INCREASING YOUR ODDS

A weapon of some sort will put you at a tactical advantage over being unarmed. We will look at a few options if you don't have access to a gun or choose not to carry one.

MACE: Mace is one of the most common less than lethal options to give you an advantage against an attacker. However, Mace as a defensive weapon is questionable. About 75 % off its effectiveness is psychological. It causes your eyes to tear up and snot to pour out of your head better than any decongestant. However, it is something that can be fought through, either by a determined attacker or one driven by a dangerous cocktail of drugs. Such people will only become more enraged by Mace, rather than deterred. Unfortunately, there is simply no way of knowing who will and won't be affected.

PEPPER SPRAY: Pepper spray, on the other hand, is 75% physical, causing dramatic burning and irritation to the person sprayed. Given the option, most times pepper spray will be more effective on an assailant. Both pepper spray and mace gives you a 5 to 10 foot distance from an attacker, which does make it useful as a non-lethal weapon. The significant downside is that about 14% of the population is not dramatically affected by either option. To police officers either is a useful tool to try to subdue an intoxicated or unruly suspect, but cops also have other force options readily available. If you chose Mace or pepper spray as your primary means of defense you need to understand the limitations of both and be prepared to strike if the nonlethal option fails.

STUN GUNS: Stun guns are effective, but, like knives, require you to be in close contact with an opponent. One of the primary benefits of a weapon is to give you distance from a threat. Stun guns that combine both a flashlight and a stun feature do offer a tool with dual effectiveness that is worth considering.

TASER: A similar defensive weapon is the Taser. Tasers launch two barbs that send 50,000 volts through the attacker to complete a circuit. Tasers work on the same general concept as a stun gun, but they add distance to the equation and complete a larger electrical circuit in the body. Most commercially available Tasers are effective out to 25 feet. While stun guns cause a localized jolt, Tasers have a larger spread, commonly locking up a person's entire body for a 5 to 15 second cycle. They are highly practical tools for law enforcement, but as a self-defense tool are limited. I've witnessed subjects remain highly combative through multiple cycles of the Taser. The problem is there are no guarantees that both barbs make a good connection with the person. Certain clothing, such as thick bubble coats, can prevent a good contact with the skin. Most Tasers allow only a single shot, however some newer models do allow for 3 separate shots. Tasers are quite simply one of the most significant developments in the past twenty years for police officers and their effectiveness has saved many lives that would have required deadly force a generation ago. Just recognize that like other less than lethal options there remain limitations. It is an electronic device, meaning sometimes buttons get pushed and nothing happens. It's not a good feeling to confront someone with a knife, pulling the trigger and nothing happens. If the Taser fails to have an immediate effect you must be prepared to carry out alternative defensive actions.

These non-lethal or less than lethal weapons are items to consider based on your local laws and your own willingness to harm another human being. This is something to seriously consider if you are thinking about what to do for your own personal security. Humans are not psychologically built to kill other humans. As we covered before, less than 3 % of the world population would be classified as psychopaths or sociopaths, where they simply feel no emotion at the prospect of taking the life of another. You need to determine how far you are willing to go while you're not under the stress of the moment to make educated decision as to the best options to protect yourself and your family. Always remember that when someone attacks you, they are not just attacking you, but also your children and any other family member that cares for you. If you are hurt or killed, that causes harm not just to you, but also to those that you love. Are you willing to fight or kill for those you love?

If you find yourself coming to the conclusion that even in the worst of circumstances you are still a pacifist, it's good to recognize that about yourself now. With that understanding you can choose the means of defense that will work best for you and your own conscience.

IMPROVISED WEAPONS

FLASHLIGHTS: Good, low cost flashlights are useful tools to always have available at hand. Flashlights give you both the ability to see what you are dealing with, but also the ability to blind an opponent. Most tactical flashlights with LEDs are far brighter than a typical flashlight of only a few years ago and also come with a jagged edge for smashing glass that can be just as useful as a slashing weapon. Those that have a strobe effect can be used to disorient an opponent in low light situations. In addition, the mere act of clinching a flashlight in your fist helps overcome the effects of vasoconstriction while reinforcing your hand, making any strike more effective.

Flashlights add concentrated force to any strike with the benefit of hitting with a solid object. Striking with a fist on a hard object, particularly if you are not trained, can lead to broken fingers or a sprained wrist. Boxers tightly wrap their hands to protect themselves against both. You are unlikely to have similar protection for your hands, so consider any object that can be used to provide focused power against a target that also prevents injury to yourself.

PENS, COMBS, KEYS: Pens in a similar manner are able to concentrate the energy of a blow to a very precise area, increasing the effectiveness of a strike. A comb, with rough teeth, can effectively rip at the soft tissue of an attacker's neck or face. Keys can be clenched in the fist, protruding through your fingers creating an ad hoc set of brass knuckles.

STICKS: Any stick, whether a 7-inch Kubotan to a 6-foot staff gives you a mechanical advantage over being unarmed. The longer the weapon the more effectively you can keep someone at a distance. However, the greater the length of the weapon the higher the level of skill you need to wield it. A 6-foot staff is rarely swung from one end, which would allow you to take full advantage of its length. Instead they are held from the center, using only the ends to strike. In general, anything over 3 feet long rapidly becomes unwieldy to an untrained person.

Even a magazine, rolled up tightly, can become an improvised striking device. It can be swung like a club, used to smash, or to jab at the throat or eyes. However, if you find yourself using a copy of the Weekly World News to fight off an attack you've probably made a mistake in either preparing for or being alert for a threat.

BUG SPRAY: Wasp and bee killer can also be used very effectively to discourage an attacker. The blast can reach out to 25 feet and the stream is far more powerful than the typical can of mace or pepper spray that is only effective to about 10 feet. Wasp spray can make breathing difficult, and without treatment, can lead to blindness. It is a last ditch type of weapon, but certainly an option to consider when thinking of items that can be effective turned into defensive tools when around the house.

SHOOTING SKILLS

A man's rights rest in three boxes: the ballot box, the jury box, and the cartridge box.

- Frederick Douglass

"The rifle itself has no moral stature, since it has no will of its own. Naturally, it may be used by evil men for evil purposes, but there are more good men than evil, and while the latter cannot be persuaded to the path of righteousness by propaganda, they can certainly be corrected by good men with rifles."

— Jeff Cooper, *Art of the Rifle*

I understand the debate over gun control and those that take a strong stance against guns and gun ownership. Most are concerned people who have never wanted a gun, have never come in contact with one, and can never understand why anyone would want one. When they hear news reports of gun violence in the street their immediate reaction is to simply outlaw guns. To their view of the world, only outlaws have guns.

This makes up the vast majority of gun control advocates. They are sincere, good-natured people who see the problem of gun violence as simple enough to solve by simply eliminating the problem of guns. However, within this group, is also a very small number that wants to disarm the public, but for other reasons. This small group is in positions of political power and they understand one thing very clearly, if they are the only ones who can have the guns, by limiting them to only agents of the government, they will never lose their power. When the people become victims of someone else's aggression they have to turn to those in power to defend them. This group stirs up the fears of those sincerely against gun ownership not out of concern for life, but so that they can remain in control. This process is repeated time and time again throughout history and through all cultures. In medieval Europe only the nobility were armed, making up the class of knights that could easily control the peasants that worked the king's land. In Japan the Samurai were a different class from the farmers, who were not even allowed to look at a Samurai without running the risk of being cut down for such disobedience. In the South, freed slaves were not allowed to own guns to defend their families, making them easy prey to hostile Whites. In modern Somalia, warlords control the streets with automatic weapons, hoarding the food and medical supplies shipped from the US and meant for the starving peasants.

The thing that made the United States unique is it did not set out separate classes of people, but rather saw all men as created equal by their Creator. This meant that we aren't set in groups, but rather as individuals. We each are given individual rights and among these is the right to defend ourselves. This is important, because when a critical event happens there is very little time to react, let alone wait for the police to respond.

I've been in situations where officers were in active gunfights, hearing them call for assistance on the radio at the moment it's occurring. Even running lights and sirens to respond to the scene, the likelihood of arriving while the shots are still flying is highly unlikely. For a civilian it's far worse as they attempt to call for help by dialing 911. There is simply too much delay in people calling the police, the dispatcher getting the information out, and the officer arriving on the scene to catch a criminal in the act. This provides little comfort to an individual who is fighting for their life. However, a person carrying a concealed handgun can immediately prevent a dangerous encounter from becoming something worse. To our nation's founders, it was obvious that you had a right to defend your own life.

Those people that believe guns are the problem simply can't recognize the problem is criminal intent, not the weapon used. When England confiscated handguns, violent crimes spiked up 40%. In the US, the cities known for strict gun control are also known as the most dangerous and violent cities, leading the country in gun deaths. **Any laws that put a limit on good people being able to protect themselves or their family only benefits criminals.**

Clearly there are a lot of very well-meaning people that believe in gun control, but ultimately you have to examine who the people are that are pushing that agenda or funding it. Is their interest to eliminate guns, or simply eliminate your access to them? When gun control advocates surround themselves with armed guards you have to question their motives. After all, they are saying you can't use force to defend yourself, but they can. They will argue they know that there are crazy people out there with guns so they have to have armed guards. Surprisingly, that's exactly the same argument of the gun rights advocates.

Good people don't need laws limiting their access to weapons. When weapons are removed from the hands of the common man, then only those that don't abide by the law and the government have the control over the use of force. This repeatedly leads to a loss of liberty for the people and an oppressive leadership to control the criminals.

The temperance movement that led to making liquor illegal looked at the world from a similar mindset. The argument then, much as it is today, is that much of society's ills stem from an over consumption of alcohol. The natural reaction was to make all alcohol illegal. But, what the proponents failed to realize, is that such laws penalized everyone for the actions of a small minority. Ultimately, this led to a vast underground network of gin joints and speakeasies and the largest crime wave in U.S. history, as illegal booze became big business and fed the rapid growth of the mafia. This eventually led to a repeal of the law, making it clear that not everyone should be charged with the actions of a few. The truth is, most gun violence is committed by as little as .03% of the population. How does it make sense to take away guns from 99.97% of the people for the crimes of so few? This would only give greater power to that small minority that relies of force and violence to get what they want.

Virtually all active shooter situations have ended due to someone with a gun arriving on the scene to end the carnage. The armed person, whether law enforcement or a citizen, either ended the threat themselves, or caused the shooter to turn his gun on himself rather than loose the crazed game he was playing. Trying to outlaw guns would only take the tool from the good guys, while the bad guys would continue to access black market guns or choose other weapons. The recent beheading of a woman in Oklahoma and a second woman stabbed shows that evil people aren't limited in what they use as a weapon. However, what stopped the attack was a coworker who was also an auxiliary deputy who used his pistol to stop the threat. A hatchet attack in New York on police officers was also ended by the use of a handgun.

As we discussed earlier, street criminals think in terms of immediate needs, they don't make long-term plans. If they are juveniles or Life Course Persistent criminals their frontal cortex development may even prevent them from making anything but emotionally based actions. That means they aren't deterred by a long prison sentence that may happen if they get caught. That concept is too far in the future and not tangible. However, **an armed victim poses an immediate deterrent because a simple robbery has suddenly become very risky.**

A week before I wrote this, a report came into our information desk that said a delivery driver was taking a pizza to a house when three thugs came around the house and demanded his money. The driver had a CCW license and immediately drew his pistol. The three robbers suddenly had a change of heart. This would not have ended so quickly or on a positive note if the delivery driver were not armed.

The truth is that such situations are all too common, though rarely reported. In this case the robbery was prevented by the victim merely brandishing his weapon and not by firing it. Generally this means a report is not taken. The only reason he called in the event was to make the police aware that the subjects were in the area and might attack someone else.

The Uniform Crime Report from 2011 shows only 653 justifiable homicides occurring that year. Police officers accounted for 393 of that number and private citizens only 260. Good people with guns is not a threat to society, it is a deterrent threat to criminals. What this shows is that there is not an epidemic of law-abiding people killing people to protect themselves. In fact, Wright and Rossi's research of convicted felons showed that they feared armed victims more than the police. The states with the highest levels of gun ownership also showed the greatest deterrent effect on the criminals (Wright & Rossi, 1986).

In Criminal Justice there's a concept known as the Criminal Justice Funnel. The idea is that only about half of all crimes ever get reported, meanings that only about 50% of crimes ever enter the top of the funnel. Of those that enter, most are cleared through dismissal, minor fines, or a night in jail. Only the most severe of crimes, usually crimes of violence, fall to the narrow portion of the funnel. Once all the crimes are shuffled through the CJ Funnel, only about 2% of the crimes that are reported ever lead to prison time. Most of the population doesn't understand that, but criminals do.

When you see the likelihood of a criminal going to prison you begin to see why prison isn't a significant deterrent to criminal behavior. The odds still remain in the criminal's favor. **The most likely way to prevent criminal actions is by hardening your property and presenting yourself as a threat.** Having a gun, and the responsibility to possess it, allows you to be that immediate threat criminals avoid.

The Crime Prevention Research Center recently found that the number of people with concealed carry permits has more than doubled over the past seven years, while murder and violent crime rates have fallen by 22%. This doesn't mean that CCWs have been the sole cause of the decline, but it does make it clear that allowing law-abiding people to carry handguns does not cause violence to skyrocket. Instead, it appears to have just the opposite effect. The CPRC's research found that for each 1% increase of the population that holds a CCW license there was a 1.4% decrease in the number of murders.

John Lott, the founder of the Crime Prevention Research Center, said "When you allow people to carry concealed handguns, you see changes in the behavior of criminals." What that means is that, "Some criminals stop committing crimes, others move on to crimes in which they don't come into contact with victims and others actually move to areas where they have less fear of being confronted by armed victims. (Klimas, 2014)"

For the past two decades violent crime has decreased consistently despite an increase in law abiding citizens arming themselves. Robberies have declined from 6.3 per 1000 people in 1994 to only 2.6 per 1000 in 2005 in the United States. Over the same period, robberies have increased in England where the population has been disarmed. It seems clear that disarming the population leads only to emboldened criminals not a safer society.

CHOOSING A GUN

Fear no man no matter his size, call on me, I will equalize.

- Advertising slogan for the Colt Peacemaker

I understand that the debate over gun control will continue. However, for those that choose to arm themselves, the larger debate is over the best caliber handgun to carry. The motto of the firearms training center Front Sight sums it up nicely, "Any gun will do, if you will do." That is really the truth of the matter. **It doesn't matter what tool you use as long as you are both capable and willing to use it to defend yourself or others. First and foremost you must arm yourself with a combat mindset.**

With that understanding there are a few things to consider. A gun is only effective if it is within arm's reach. Outside of that, you are unarmed fighting to get to your weapon. Because of that, you should consider a weapon that is compact enough to have readily available and on you at virtually all times.

However, as you consider convenience, you also have to consider that no one ever entered into a gunfight thinking, "Jeez, I wish I had brought a smaller gun with less ammunition." Here in lies the real paradox in choosing to carry a concealed firearm. It must be both convenient and small enough for consistent daily carry, but large enough to be a combat proven caliber and hold enough rounds to present a credible threat.

Also, extremely small (pocket) pistols are often viewed as girl's guns, but they are far more difficult to shoot quickly and accurately than larger guns by males and females alike. Small pistols are often called a gut gun, where its effective range is only close enough to jab it into an attacker's gut and pull the trigger. Because of their diminutive size there is little of the gun to absorb the recoil of a shot and far less of a grip to hold onto, limiting a person's ability to effectively control the kick. Women who start with such a small gun often shy away from guns altogether because of the recoil. Most people will find a larger gun far easier to control as well as more effective at ending a fight.

However, a full size handgun that works fine for a 10 hour shift for a police officer in a duty belt, quickly becomes too large and cumbersome to wear comfortably while out with your family. A rifle or shotgun might be even more effective and intimidating, but sling one over your shoulder and head out to McDonalds to get some chicken nuggets and things might not play out well. If your only option is a larger gun, it all too frequently means that the gun is simply left at home. It is not a good feeling to be put in a situation where you could have stopped a threat to your family, but you couldn't because you decided it wasn't convenient.

With the benefit of modern gun designs the best guns for concealed carry are a compact, or sub compact version of a full size handgun. Of these the Glock 19 represents a nice balance. It is smaller than the full size Glock 17, but is often carried by law enforcement officers as their primary weapon. However, it's smaller size makes if reasonably comfortable to wear on a daily basis by civilians or by police in undercover assignments.

For an even smaller design the "Baby Glock" Model 26 has become to standard-bearer for concealed carry ever since it was first introduced 20 years ago. Although small, it will accept the magazines of larger Glocks, but will hold 10 rounds in its own magazine.

Glocks remain the dominant handgun in law enforcement, with 65% of agencies relying on some version of a Glock. They are simple and extremely reliable, both critical in a life and death incident. Having carried concealed handguns both on and off duty for well over a decade; both models represent a good balance for what to look for as a concealed carry handgun.

Smith and Wesson's M&P compact models are also a great option for concealed carry. Like the Glock, the M&P compact has a double stack magazine. This allows for more rounds, but also makes for a wider gun. To address the need for a thinner gun that is easier for day-to-day carry, S&W developed the Shield. The S&W Shield is almost identical in dimensions to the compact, but has a single stack magazine, making it thinner and easier to carry with light clothing during the summer.

The narrow size of a single stack pistol is important when you consider that the pistol holster will also add bulk. A double stack pistol is quite wide, and once a quality leather holster is wrapped around it, things do become quite cumbersome. Whichever pistol you prefer, carry it consistently in the same place and in the same holster. If you move the weapon from a jacket pocket one day, to your hip the next, to a front pocket the next will only make your reaction time slower under stress. You will naturally react to where you most commonly keep the pistol. For most circumstances, the quickest and most consistent way of carrying a concealed weapon is with an inside the pants holster covered by a shirt or jacket.

I mentioned Glock and S&W to give you an idea of an ideal pistol size that is both large enough to easily control and small enough to carry everyday without discomfort. Certainly there are other well-known manufactures that produce quality handguns that you may prefer. However, whatever you choose, look for safe action pistol designs such as those mentioned. Safe action handguns have built in safety devices that prevent them from firing unless a finger is on the trigger. There is no external safety to have to manipulate. Along with carrying the pistol consistently in the same location, under the stress of a gunfight fine motor skills become difficult. Each additional action you have to take to make your pistol function, such as flipping a safety, is one more thing that can go wrong when your life is on the line. The less you have to think about the more effective you will react under stress.

CALIBER

Truth be told, the .45 remains the most effective stopping round that can be shot comfortably from a handgun. A .44 or larger has even more stopping force, but is difficult to control or to stow away in your Speedo at the beach. The 9MM remains the most common of defensive handguns and generally allows for several more rounds to be carried in the magazine than a .45. The 9MM has many detractors as it has lacked power and often required multiple hits to vital areas to stop a threat. The 9MM is similar in size to the .38 caliber pistol rounds carried by British soldiers during the Boar war. The English soldiers found that .38 caliber bullets did little to stop the advances of Sulu warriors, who were drugged up on powerful narcotics, while the .45 could have stopped the threat immediately. However, with modern self-defense rounds, the difference between .45 and 9MM becomes increasingly less significant, making proper shot placement more critical than the caliber of the weapon.

Before purchasing a gun it makes sense to rent or borrow a model that you're interested in buying and shooting it several times to get an idea of how comfortable you will be with the gun. If possible, shoot several different models back to back to compare the pros and cons of each. My wife recently shot a S&W compact, Shield, and a S&W Bodyguard at a target range. Within an hour she could consistently hit headshots at 10 yards with the compact. She was almost equally effective with the Shield. However, even at seven yards, she found the diminutive .380 Bodyguard difficult to get anywhere close to her point of aim. The ability to compare what works best for you is important before you commit to something that you end up feeling uncomfortable shooting or unwilling to carry.

Stance

During the range time it also became clear that my wife suffered a common issue among novice shooters that leads to frequent malfunctions. She consistently had stove pipes and double feeds as the slide attempted to eject a spent shell and prepare the next round. She was suffering from 'limp-wristing' the gun, allowing her wrists to break up and back with the recoil. This minor mistake prevents the gun's slide to properly strip the first round and replace the next. This is corrected simply by keeping the wrists, elbows, and shoulders firmly locked, allowing the slide to move straight back and the recoil to be driven back into the shoulders, rather than the wrists or elbows.

She was able to overcome the limp-wristing by a change in grip and stance. The stance that proves consistently to be both the quickest way to engage targets effectively and recover faster for follow-up shots in real life combat is the isosceles stance. It is a natural stance that people tend to revert to under the stress of a gunfight even if they train to target shoot in a different manner.

The isosceles stance involves placing the feet shoulder width apart with the upper body breaking slightly forward at the waist, leaning towards the threat. Both arms lock out straight in front of your eyes with the weak, or support, hand wrapped around the gun hand. The thumb of the gun hand should lay directly on top of the support thumb, both pointing down the frame of the gun and directly towards the target.

This stance has proven itself effective in competition and in combat for several reasons. The locking of the arms and leaning forward allows the recoil to go straight back and into the upper body, rather than forcing the arms to fight the recoil alone. This allows for quicker recovery after each shot. Pointing the thumbs straight down the slide toward the target allows the shooter to acquire an almost perfect sight alignment simply by pointing the thumbs towards the threat. Once in the position, the arms remain locked and the eyes stay on the front sight. To move to another threat, the body pivots at the waist, moving the entire upper body as a unit, much like a tank turret rotating from side to side. This creates a solid, consistent shooting platform that can rapidly engage multiple targets without changing focus on the front sight.

This stance also allows for your eyes to quickly pick up the sights as you confront a threat. It requires most people a quarter second to a full second to focus from a target to their front sight, depending on the distance from the threat. By adopting the isosceles stance, the sight is placed instinctively in front of your eyes. If you pull the gun straight back, the sight remains on the target. As you push back out, the sight remains on the target. This is called 'riding the rail', and allows you to rapidly engage a threat as you draw from concealment.

As your gun hand draws the weapon, your support hand comes to the middle of your chest. Your gun hand comes up to the support hand and they both push straight out, 'riding the rail' towards the target. This allows you to be engaging your threat even before you reach full extension or a perfect sight picture. If you 'ride the rail' back, bringing the gun back to the chest, you are now holding the pistol in a 'high ready', allowing you to still engage a threat while keeping the weapon out of arms reach of a nearby opponent.

With the proper stance in place, there are three other fundamentals that make for consistent and rapid shot placement.

Breathing - Take in a deep breath as you draw your pistol and allow a long slow breath out as you acquire your target. This helps steady your nerves and your sights. **Don't hold your breath**. This is a practiced skill. Under stress you will naturally inhale and hold, forgetting to breathe.

Front sight - Everything else is secondary. The front sight is your point of focus, with the rear sight and the target slightly blurred. The top of the front sight is even and centered within the rear sight, and placed dead center on the spot you intend to shoot. Remain focused on the front sight. Under the stress of real combat you may not have a perfect sight picture, but if you are focused on the front sight and it is squarely placed in the chest of your attacker, there are few places for your rounds can go other than in him.

Trigger press - A smooth press on the trigger straight back, not anticipating the trigger break or the recoil. There should be a surprise trigger break, where the pistol fires before you expect it to. If you anticipate the trigger break you will find yourself consistently shooting low. At short distances it appears minor. At 25 yards it's off target. This is best practiced with dry firing the pistol, or practicing with Air Soft or BB versions of your chosen pistol. You simply practice pressing back on the trigger while maintaining a consistent sight picture.

If you practice these four fundamentals of pistol craft: proper stance, breathing, focusing on the front sight, and smooth trigger press you will see consistent and rapid shots on target.

DEFENDING YOUR HOME

At home you are not under the same limitations with a gun as you are if you choose to carry a pistol concealed. To defend your home, the ability to quickly access the biggest gun you can bring to the party is really your choice to make. Granted, it has to be a caliber that you are comfortable and effective with, but concealment and practicality is not your primary concern.

What you do need to consider for home defense is if you are retreating to a safe location and defending yourself, or will you be in a situation where you must move through your house to protect your family. Ultimately, that will define your decision in what weapon to choose.

If you plan to defend yourself in a safe room or in your bedroom, seeking cover behind a locked door and your mattress a shotgun would be a good first choice. A twelve-gauge pump shotgun loaded with 00 buckshot will send 9 rounds of .32 caliber pellets towards any threat that is unfortunate enough to come through the door. In the close confines of a house, the shots won't scatter much more broadly than 6 inches, but allows for less precision and more stopping power than a pistol. The mere racking of the slide will send all but the most determined intruders the other way. The shot also is less likely to penetrate through multiple walls like a rifle round or a slug, making it more desirable when you don't know what might lie beyond your target.

Lesser shotgun loads, such as birdshot, are so light that they might not even penetrate a heavy jacket. If you think that you would prefer injuring someone, without running the risk of killing him or her when using a shotgun, then you've made a poor decision. As I mentioned before, if you point a gun at someone, you are making the decision that you may have to kill that person in order to stop a threat. That means choosing a round capable of ending the fight decisively. Former Vice President Dick Cheney shot an elderly shooting companion in the face with birdshot during a hunting accident, but caused only minor injuries. There are two things to learn from this. First, if birdshot only caused minor injury to an elderly person it is unlikely to stop an aggressive opponent. Secondly, don't go hunting with Dick Cheney.

If you need to move through your house, a shotgun becomes a bit unwieldy. Doors have to be opened, and two hands are required to use a shotgun or rifle effectively. When moving through a house a pistol will tend to be easier to wield, allowing the weak hand to open doors, while your dominant hand pulls the weapon back to your chest in a 'high ready' to prevent it from being taken if someone is just behind the door.

Before opening a door, position yourself along the wall near the doorknob. Whether the door pushes in or opens out, standing on the side of the knob allows you to not lean your body in front of the door to open it, nor be distracted by the door as it opens. You want to position yourself to be able to see down the length of the wall directly behind the door. The only portion of the wall you won't be able to see is the corner itself.

As you peer into the room, step back at least an arm's length from the doorway and take a very small step to the side, allowing you to see slightly more of the room. As you see a segment of the room is clear, take another small step to see more of the room. This is known as "cutting the pie", moving slowly to reveal more and more of a room or a corridor. The movement involves the foot leading and the head, body, and gun following as a unit. For obvious reasons you don't want to lead with your head.

Following this technique you can see a room's entire interior except for the corners of the closest wall. This prevents you from moving into an unknown situation and having a good understanding where someone is most likely hiding in a room.

If you need to move forward into a room you need to do so quickly. The doorway is a "fatal funnel" that silhouettes you as a target the longer you remain there. As you enter a room your movement should be decisive and down the near wall, quickly determining if there is a threat in the corner you are moving towards and sweeping over the room as you move.

This description of moving through your home makes it clear that you need to move quickly and to be able to manipulate doors with your free hand. For this reason, if you can only afford one gun, or prefer to have only one for defensive purpose, a compact handgun of the largest caliber you can comfortably carry is your best choice. It offers both stopping power and the ability to have it on you wherever you are. The safest place to keep a gun even in you residence is on you. Clint Eastwood once said he believed in gun control. If there's a gun in the room he wants to control it. It's a good rule to live by. If you have a pistol on you the odds in a fight will tilt in your favor. There is a valid reason that the Colt Peacemaker was called the great equalizer during the Old West; it gave everyone equal footing.

For both safety and immediate access to your defensive tool, having a pistol on you is the only reasonable course of action. A threat at the rear door while you're in your kitchen and your pistol or shotgun is in the bedroom is not an effective defense. A gun outside of arm's reach means that you are effectively unarmed and fighting your way to the gun. Even if you get to a gun in the bedroom will it be secured with a lock or in a safe? How long will it take to access it under stress?

With that in consideration, again consider a handgun that you are comfortable having on you almost all the time even at home. Most defensive shooting situations will be within 7 yards, making most compact handguns accurate enough to be on target.

FLASHLIGHTS

Most gun battles occur at night. That brings up the significance of having a flashlight and learning to use it in conjunction with a gun. Moving with a gun and flashlight at night is done by clicking on the light for a moment to see your surroundings before turning it off and moving under the cover of darkness. You don't want to leave the light on to highlight your position or your movements, only to identify and blind your opponent while you gain your bearings. Any movement you make should be concealed from an attacker.

If you carry a flashlight, rather than a weapon mounted version, you need to find a means of holding both that is both effective at gaining a sight picture and supporting the gun. For years the FBI taught a technique of holding the flashlight high above you or out to the side with the weak hand to draw fire towards the light and away from your body. It was a reasonable thought in theory, but in reality it becomes difficult to effectively highlight the target with the flashlight while getting a sight picture with the gun.

A two handed position that allows the hand with the flashlight to offer support for the weapon makes for better control and faster target acquisition This can be accomplished by placing the flashlight alongside the pistol, resting your flashlight hand against your weapon hand, largely mimicking the isosceles stance covered earlier. This allows you to light exactly what you are targeting with the weapon and better control the weapon during recoil. However, it does fall short of a weapon-mounted light for speed and control.

The reason a handgun is preferable when moving through a house over a rifle or shotgun, is the ability to handle doors. You can manipulate doors and pull the weapon into the body, rather than leading with the muzzle of a rifle or shotgun where it can be easily wrestled from you. However, if you try to clear a house with a flashlight in one hand and the pistol in the other, you can get the sense of how difficult it is to turn a doorknob with your weak hand while already holding a light. The more you think about it, the more a weapon mounted light makes sense.

Having a flashlight mounted to you weapon makes target acquisition and accuracy improve dramatically. You are controlling a single light weapon system and controlling it with both hands. Experiments done at our police range showed the significant difference in using a light mounted to a pistol compared to holding a flashlight in the weak hand in both speed and accuracy of fire. Flashlight mounts work.

The downside is both additional bulk and the need to point the weapon at anything to cast light on it. One of the fundamental rules of firearms safety is to avoid pointing a weapon at anything you're not willing to destroy. Having a flashlight mounted on the gun is certainly a disadvantage from a safety perspective, but in the dark it is also the best way of confirming the identity of what you're shooting at before you pull the trigger.

WHAT SHOULD YOU TARGET?

Recently one member of our city council asked why the police aren't trained to shoot guns out of criminal's hands. After all, she reasoned, she'd seen such shots in movies and television shows hundreds of times before. Thank goodness we have elected positions for people such as this, otherwise they would be forced into full care mental facilities early in life.

The simple fact is that consistent, accurate shots at a gun range can be trained. However, as we've talked about earlier, the physiological effects on your body while under stress make the ability to hit a small, moving target more the result of chance than of skill. The ability to accurately shoot an arm or leg is difficult, but also doesn't guarantee an immediate stop to an attacker's aggression. Due to vasoconstriction, it's quite possible that an attacker won't even experience pain from an initial injury in an extremity. This is the reason you must strike, or shoot, at areas that shut your opponent's body down. The police involved shooting in Ferguson, Missouri is an example of how multiple shots in a suspect's arm didn't prevent what the officer perceived as an immediate threat. That makes targeting the chest cavity as the most likely shot placement to strike a location that will quickly disable an attacker by taking out a vital organ.

As unappealing as it sounds, once you have to rely on a gun to defend yourself means that you are involved in a life and death decision. His actions must rise to the level that no other option is available to defend yourself or someone else. You shoot with the intent to stop the threat and that brings with it the possibility that one or more shots may prove fatal. Multiple shots to the arm or leg simply will not accomplish this. Even a fatal shot to the heart will not necessarily cause immediate incapacitation. People shot fatally in the heart can remain a threat for up to 5 seconds after they've been struck. Recognize that fact the next time someone asks why so many shots were fired during a police shootout. Five seconds is a long time. In fact, a 17 round clip can be emptied in that time frame if you still see the person as a threat and have no idea where, or even if, he's been hit.

The clearest way to stop a threat is to use the largest caliber you can comfortably shoot. Any caliber of .380 or smaller, almost requires a shot to the cranial-ocular cavity, essentially the triangle formed by the eyes and nose, rather than the chest to incapacitate an attacker. As these pistols are frequently small, pocket pistols, the difficulty of getting such shot placement under pressure becomes increasingly difficult.

ACTIVE SHOOTERS

Eric Harris and Dylan Klebold walked into Columbine High School set on murder. They were loaded down with 99 explosive devices and multiple firearms. They had no specific targets, only the intent to create massive carnage. By the time they were done 1 teacher and 12 students were dead and another 27 were wounded.

Although there had been hostage situations and even mass shootings in the past, their killing spree in 1999 marked the beginning of a new form of threat known as the active shooter. It also revealed how unprepared both law enforcement and civilians were to dealing with criminals who had no purpose beyond killing for its own reward.

A decade and a half has gone by since that day. Since that time more than 160 similar events have occurred in schools and businesses. A FBI study of these events in 2013 revealed the shocking reality of such violence. **The average response time for police in such incidents is 8 to 10 minutes. However, nearly 70% of the shooting sprees last less than 5 minutes.** Shooters realize that once they have committed to the event that they have a very short period of time to cause the most damage that they can.

Many police agencies rely on SWAT teams to deal with such situations. The delay in getting specialized officers and weapons to the scene only adds to the destruction of life. As a means of getting police into buildings faster some agencies developed a Quad system where a 4 to 6 member team of officers that are first on scene enter the building in a diamond formation and move towards the sound of the shooting. No one else could enter a building during this time for risk that the team would engage another officer. Although the idea was sound in both theory and tactics, it also required a significant delay as officers had to organize to enter the building.

After Columbine, Greg Cane, a police officer married to a school principal, asked what schools were doing to deal with active shooters. His wife told him that teachers and students were taught to simply lockdown the building and seek cover like they were preparing for a tornado drill. Over the course of the decade such a passive responses by victims revealed one very clear fact that Cane recognized instinctively - **hiding in a corner or under a desk only causes you to be a sitting target.** In the case of the Columbine shooting, 10 of the children killed were hiding under desks in the library. Both Harris and Klebold simply stood at one end of the library sadistically picking off each new victim.

Cane developed a system that involved fleeing, fighting, or barricading yourself against an active threat. Cane's idea was dismissed by Homeland Security for much of the decade, while they continued to advise teachers to lockdown, hide, and wait for the police. However, despite the suggestion of the feds, some people forced into these situations were taking action against the killers and it was working. A consistent pattern showed that a teacher, principal, or a citizen simply confronting the shooter brought an end the threat in 13% of all active shooter crimes. They effectively became guardians of the location rather than victims. The rest ended only after the shooter knew that police were in the building and were closing in on his position, making them take their own life or forcing the police to do so. From all of the events, what was proving to consistently end the killing was someone willing to confront the threat.

Eight years after Columbine, Seung-Hui Cho shot and killed 2 people in a Virginia Tech dorm before moving across campus to Norris Hall. Cho locked 3 of the entrance with chains and began a killing spree that was on par with the goriest video game. After 9 minutes he had fired 174 rounds, killing 30 and wounding another 23. He turned the gun on himself only after he heard police enter through a door he had not secured.

Although there were a significantly larger number of people killed at Virginia Tech than Columbine years before a far greater percentage survived. They survived simply by barricading the door to their room or by jumping from windows. This active, rather than passive, approach to dealing with an active shooter proved to be critical in dealing with the attack. It was only after Virginia Tech that the feds began to see that there might be something to Greg Cane's ideas of active resistance.

The model he developed is called ALICE: Alert, Lockdown, Inform, Counter, and Evacuate.

ALERT - Advise everyone in the area what is happening in clear language. The goal is to make everyone in the danger zone aware of what is happening so they can make their own decision in how to react. They are not required to act in any specific way, but need to be made aware of what is happening so they can decide upon a reasonable course of action.

LOCKDOWN - Unlike like traditional views of lockdowns, which often endangered students, the new view was set up barricades in front of doors to force a shooter working on limited time to move on to an easier target, only to find other targets equally barricaded. After students make sure an entrance to a room is well barricaded they can make a plan to counter or escape the threat.

INFORM - If someone has an idea of where the shooter or shooters are they need to get that information out. If a shooter is in the front hallway and people are aware of it, there is no reason to stay put at the rear of the building, waiting for the shooter like in traditional lockdowns. Those away from the threat should be attempting to escape by any means necessary.

COUNTER - Any distraction that reduces a killer's movements and ability to target people is allowed. Throwing books, swinging chairs, or using fire extinguishers are all acceptable reactions that cause the shooter to move or be struck. This significantly decreases the number of people he can harm and may even overwhelm him.

EVACUATE - Under stress the natural reaction is either fight or flight. In a situation where the threat is better armed, fleeing makes logical sense. Trained law enforcement officers, at best have a 20% hit probability in an active gunfight. However, active shooters have a 50% kill probability, simply because they are typically shooting at a stationary and non-confrontational target. Running from a shooter decreases the likelihood of being shot to only 4%. If you can get out of an environment with an active shooter then go.

The thought behind ALICE is to do what is necessary to survive. You are taking action to make others aware of the threat, to make it more difficult to get to you, to fight back, or to run. You can do all these steps, or go straight to running. But it entails recognizing that in a critical incident there is not enough time to wait for the police. **You have to be the first responder and do what is necessary to improve the likelihood that you and others survive.**

FINAL THOUGHTS

The active shooter is the last topic of this book for one simple reason. The lessons learned over the past decade and a half involving over 160 active shooter incidents validate everything else that we've covered in the previous chapters. **By the time the police arrive nearly 75% of crimes are already over. The simple reality is that police don't prevent crime, they more often than not respond to investigate crime.**

To prevent crime you need to take steps to target harden both yourself and your property. You don't have to make something impenetrable; it simply needs to be difficult enough that a burglar, robber, or an active shooter decides that the risk is not worth their effort. This can often be accomplished by making your home or apartment more difficult to access and to make you appear to be alert and confident.

Ultimately being alert and aware are both fundamental in avoiding dangerous situations. If you are informed of the potential risks around you the odds of being a victim diminish. Simply knowing that roughly 3% of locations in your city account for half of all crime will help you decrease your odds of being victimized simply by avoiding those spots. Often this information can be found on local crime sites or simply by watching the news and seeing what locations constantly make the news. If you are in a location that makes you feel uncomfortable there is something about the environmental design that is causing you to feel nervous. Those same design elements that trigger your 'Spidey sense' will only give confidence to a criminal. Once that feeling of dread happens AVOID the location if you can. If you can't, be ALERT.

If you remain alert you can simply get out of the area and avoid possible confrontations. However, if you must fight back, fight back aggressively. A criminal expects and depends on a helpless victim. If you prove to be aggressive and combative they are unlikely to be prepared to fight you off.

For a crime to happen there are three elements that must come together - a location, offender, and a victim. Remove any one of these elements and a crime cannot occur. Each side of the triangle of crime is watched over by someone. A manager controls a location; probation officers or family members control offenders; and guardians protect victims. In protecting your home, you are the manager and your decisions directly determine how much and what type of crime can occur at your residence. This is not limited to just locks and lights, but to the people that you allow into your life. The FBI's Uniform Crime Report from 2011 indicate that 54% of all murders are committed by an offender the victim knew and roughly 1/3 are committed by a family member. Those numbers are likely to be higher as some murders go unsolved. What's important to realize is that you have the ability to manage how your residence is protected and whom you allow into your life. This gives you the ability to control the amount and type of crime that occurs at your home. When you are away from your home you have two options, you can be a victim in an environment, or you can choose to be a guardian. The decision you make can significantly impact if a crime can even happen to you or someone else while at a location.

Although this book covers using aggressive, simple techniques to stop a physical assault, the intent behind the book is decidedly anti-violence. Only a very small percentage of the population is violent and they tend to interact with people of a violent nature. A good person recognizes proper authority and has the character to avoid meaningless confrontations. However, a good person willing to act violently to defend others is what keeps the wolves in society at bay. Lt. Col. David Grossman refers to the people willing to react aggressively as sheepdogs. It's the sheepdogs that make it their responsibility to protect those around them. They don't have to be police or military, they only have to be alert, willing to react, and capable of responding effectively. If you choose to be a sheepdog you make the world a safer place and you become a guardian in any environment you enter.

If you take steps now to properly secure your home, make good decisions on the people you deal with, and present yourself as a credible risk in your daily life your likelihood of being victimized will be greatly diminished. If you adopt a few of the things you have learned and follow only a few relatively simple steps you make yourself into a Hard Target.

FOR FURTHER STUDY

The author has given every effort to acknowledge the researchers and their work referenced throughout this book. The intent is to give credit to the originator of the concepts and to provide additional information to readers that are interested in further knowledge on a concept.

Most of the research articles cited and found in the reference section are available in pdf form on the Internet. Although some studies require access to an academic library, others are readily available through a simple Google search. Enter the researcher's name and the title of the article to find out more.

The sections of this book focused on armed and unarmed self-defense stem from a decade of training in the martial art and fifteen years of law enforcement training. Much of what is shared is information passed on from various instructors throughout the years. However, I would suggest that if you would like further information on unarmed self-defense you should consider Debbie Gardner of the Survival Institute, Tim Larkin's Target Focus Training, or Damian Ross' Self Defense Company. All focus on simple, effective strikes to vital areas to end a violent encounter.

If you want to train with a qualified instructor, I highly recommend that you look for someone near you that teaches Krav Maga. I am a fan of all martial arts and you can benefit from any training, however many have a focus on sport and discipline rather than defense. Many styles developed as warriors tried to maintain their skills when combat was no longer a necessity. Krav Maga, on the other hand, developed as a necessity for Israeli troops constantly facing combat in the field today. Because of that, Krav Maga takes out all but the most fundamental movements and uses the same defense against multiple attacks, increasing your reaction speed. While grappling is great in the ring, in combat it will get you killed. To understand this concept better look up video from the series Human Weapon under Krav Maga. You will quickly realize why it's a bad idea to try to tie someone up with your grappling and wrestling skills. Doing so only makes it easier for him to stab you to death.

If you choose to arm yourself with a handgun, I suggest training at Ignatius Piazza's Front Sight to learn gun safety and proper skill at arms. If this school isn't feasible, I highly recommend that you seek training from a certified NRA instructor. You will learn both how to safely handle a firearm and to develop the skill necessary to use one confidently.

To find out more about Crime Prevention Through Environmental Design (CPTED), look up Oscar Newman's research called Creating Defensible Space. It is available for free at http://defensiblespace.com/book.htm. His research gives a good overview of what CPTED is, why it works, and how it can be used in various locations.

For a better understanding of most crimes and the means of combatting them I also suggest The Center for Problem Oriented Policing at http://www.popcenter.org/. This website is free and offers an almost limitless resource for dealing with crime for both the police and community members.

About the Author

Brent Adams is a police supervisor in a major city police department, having served in uniform, bike, and old clothes assignments. He holds a Masters Degree in Criminal Justice, specializing in Law Enforcement and Crime Prevention. He studied and taught Budo-taijutsu (ninjutsu) for a decade with the bruises to prove it.

References

•Anderson, J. (2015) Home Defense Tactics. ISCQC Extreme Survival Series.

  CQC International, Inc.

•Bak, P. (1999). Self-organized criticality: A holistic view of nature. In

  G.Cowan,D. Pines and D. Meltzer (Eds.),Complexity: Metaphors,

  models, and reality. Cambridge, MA: Perseus Books.

•Bandura, A. (1977). Social Learning Theory. New York: General Learning

  Press

•Berkley, B. J. (1997). Preventing customer altercations in nightclubs.

  Cornell Hotel and Restaurant Administration Quarterly, 38(2), 82-94.

•Bittner, E. (1970). The functions of the police in modern society. National

  Institute of   Mental Health.

•Bittner, E. (1980). Florence Nightingale in pursuit of Willie Sutton: A theory of the police. pp.

  119-147 in E. Bittner (Author), *The Functions of Police in Modern Society*. Cambridge,

  MA: Oelgeschlager, Gunn, and Gain Publishers.

•Blumstein, A. & Cohen, J. (1987). Chracterizing Criminal Careers. Science

  237: 985-991.

•Braga, A. Papachristos, A. & Hureau, D. (2012): The Effects of Hot Spots

  Policing on Crime: An Updated Systematic Review and Meta-Analysis, Justice Quarterly, DOI:10.1080/07418825.2012.673632

•Brantingham, P. & Brantingham, P. (1995). Crime generators and crime

  attractors. *European Journal on Criminal Policy & Research, 3,* 5-26.

•Bayley, D.H. (1994) The myth of the police. Police for the Future. New

  York: Oxford

•Clarke, R.V. & Cornish, D. (1985). Modeling offender's decisions: A framework for research &

  policy. In *Crime & Justice: An Annual Review of Research.*

•Cohen, L., and Felson, M. (1979) Social change and crime rate trends: A

  routine activity approach. American Sociological Review vol. 44 pp.

  588– 608.

•Cohen, T.H. & Reaves, B.A. (2006). Felony Defendants in Large Urban

  Counties, 2002

•Crank, J.P., and Langworthy, R. (1992). An institutional perspective of policing. *Journal of*

  Criminal Law and Criminology, 83, 338-363.

•Cuddy, A., Wilmuth, C.A. and Carney, D.R. (2012) The Benefit of Power

       Posing Before a High-Stakes Social Evaluation. Harvard Business School Working Paper, No. 13-027, September 2012.

•DiMaggio, P.J. & Powell, W. (1983) The iron cage revisited: Institutional

       isomorphism and collective rationality in organizational fields.

       American Sociological Review. 48, 147-160

•Durkheim, E. (1893) The Division of Labour in Society.

•Eck, J.E., Clarke, R.V. and Guerette, R.T. (2007) Risky facilities: Crime concentration in

       homogeneous sets of establishments and facilities. In: G. Farrell, K.J. Bowers, S.D. Johnson and M. Townsley (eds.) Imagination for Crime

       Prevention, Crime Prevention Studies , Vol. 19 , Monsey, NY: Crime Prevention Studies, pp. 225-264.

•Eck, J. E. & Spelman, W. (1987). Problem solving: Problem-oriented

       policing in Newport News. Washington, DC: National Institute of Justice.

•Engel, R. S., Tillyer, R. & Cherkauskas, J. C. (2007). Understanding best

       search and seizure practices: Final report. Submitted to the Ohio State Highway Patrol,   Office of the Superintendent, Columbus, OH.

•Engel, R. S., Calnon, J. M., Tillyer, R., Johnson, R. R. Liu, L. & Wang, X.

       (2005). Project on police-Citizen contacts, year 2 final report. Submitted to Pennsylvania State Police, Harrisburg, PA.

•Farrell, G. and Pease, K. (1993) Once Bitten, Twice Bitten: Repeat

       Victimization and its Implications for Crime Prevention. (Crime Prevention Unit Paper 5.) London, UK: Home Office.

•Forst, B., Leahy, F., Shirhall, J., Tyson, H., Wish, E., & Bartolomeo, J.

       (1982). Arrest convictability as a measure of police performance. Washington, DC: U.S. Department of Justice.

•Forst, B., Lucianovic, J., & Cox, S. (1977).What happens after arrest?

       Washington, DC: Institute for Law and Social Research.

•Friedman, L.M. & Percival, R.V. (1981). The roots of justice. Chapel Hill,

       NC: University of North Carolina Press.

•Fisher, B.S., Sloan, J.J., Cullen, F.T., & Lu, C. (1998). Crime in the ivory

       tower: the level and sources of student victimization. Criminology. 26, 671-710

•Gardner, D. (2002). Simply the BST crime survival. BookMasters Inc.

•Goldstein, H. (1979). Improving policing: A problem-oriented approach.

       Crime and Delinquency 25:236-258.

•Gottfredson, M. R., & Gottfredson, D. M. (1988). Decision making in

       criminal justice: Toward the rational exercise of discretion, 2nd Edition. New York: Plenum Press.

•Grossman, D. & Christensen, L. (2008). On Combat, The Psychology and

       Physiology of Deadly Conflict in War and in Peace. Warrior Science Publications.

•Grossman, D. (2009). On Killing: The Psychological Cost of Learning to Kill

       in War and Society. Back Bay Books.

•Hirschi, T. (1969). Causes of Delinquency. University of California Press.

•Kelling, G.L., Et Al. (1974) - The Kansas City Preventive Patrol Experiment.

The Police Foundation.

- Kelling, G.L. & Moore, M.H. (1988) Evolving Strategy of Policing

    Washington, DC: U.S. Department of Justice.

- Kirk, D.S. and Matsuda, M. (2011). Legal Cynicism, Collective Efficacy, And

    the Ecology of Arrest. Criminology, 49: 443-472.

- Klockers, C. (1983) The Dirty Harry problem. Thinking about Police: Contemporary Readings,

    McGraw-Hill, New York. 428-438.

- Klimas, L. (2014). What One Recent Study Found About Murder Rates and

    Concealed Carry Permits Is Likely to Make Gun Owners Smile. TheBlaze.com. Jul. 10, 2014.

- Kock, R. (1999). 80-20 Principle: The secret to success by achieving more

    with less. New York: Doubleday.

- Koper, C.S. (1995). Just enough police presence: Reducing crime and

    disorderly behavior by optimizing patrol time in crime hot spots.

    Justice Quarterly, 12, 649-672

- Larkin, T. & Rank-Buhr, C. (2008) How to Survive the Most Critical 5

    Seconds of Your Life. Straitview Publishing, Sequim, WA.

- Levine, J.P. (1975) The ineffectiveness of adding police to prevent crime.

    Public Policy 23:523-45.

- Madensen, T. & Eck, J. (2008). Violence in bars: Exploring the impact of   place   manager

    decision-making. Crime Prevention and Community Safety. 10, 111-125.

- Merton, R.K. (1938). Social Structure and Anomie. American Sociological

    Review 3(5):672-682.

- Meyer, J.W. & Rowan, B (1977) -Institutional organizations: Formal

    Structure as Myth and Ceremony. American Journal of Sociology. 83,

    340-363

- Mirlees-Black, C., Mayhew, P. & Percy, A. (1996). The 1996 British Crime

    Survey: England and Wales. Research and Statistics Directorate. Home Office Statistical Bulletin Issue 1996. London: Home Office.

- Moffitt, T. (1993). Adolescence-Limited and Life-Course-Persistent

    Antisocial Behavior: A Developmental Taxonomy. Psychological Review

    Vol. 100. No. 4, 674-701.

- Mustaine, E.E. & Tewksbury, R. (1998). Predicting risks of larceny theft

    victimization: a routine activities analysis using refined lifestyle measures. Criminology. 36, 829-857

- National Crime Victimization Survey (1993) United States Department of

    Justice.

- Newman, O. (1996) Creating Defensible Space. Institute for Community

Design Analysis. U.S. Department of Housing and Urban Development Office of Policy Development and Research. Available at www.humanics-

es.com/defensible-space.pdf

•Park, R. E., Burgess, E. W., & McKenzie, R. D. (1925). *The City*. Chicago,

Illinois: The University of Chicago Press.

•Piazza, I. (2011) Front Sight Student Prep Manual. What Every Gun Owner

Should Know Before Attending a Firearms Training Course. Front Sight Firearms Training Institute.

•Schneider, S. (2010). Crime prevention: Theory and practice. New York:

CRC Press.

•Seidl, J. (2014). Former Navy SEAL on the One Piece of Advice You Need to

Protect Yourself. TheBlaze.com 4/26/14

•Sherman, L.W. (1990) Police crackdowns: Initial and residual deterrence.

In M. Tonry & N. Morris (Eds.), Crime and justice: An annual review of

research (Vol. 12). Chicago: university of Chicago Press.

•Sherman, L.W., Gartin, P.R. and Buerger, M.E. (1989). Hot spots of

predatory crime: Routine activities and the criminology of place.

Criminology 27:27-55.

•Smith, D. A. (1986). The neighborhood context of police behavior. A. J.

Reissc Jr. and Michael Tonry (eds.).*Communities and Crime*. Chicago: University of Chicago Press.

•Sparrow, M. (2008). *The character of harms. Operational challenges in control*. Cambridge

University Press.

•Spelman, W. & Brown, D.K. Calling the Police: Citizen Reporting of

Serious Crime. Washington, D.C.: National Institute of Justice, 1984.

•Terill, W. and Mastrofski, S. (2002). Situational and Officer Based

Determinats of Police Coercion. Justice Quarterly, Vo. 19(2), pp. 215-248.

•TRS Direct (2011) Alpha Signals. Fightfast.com.

•Uniform Crime Report (2011) Federal Bureau of Investigation.

•US Department of Justice. Bureau of Justice Statistics. Criminal

victimization in the United States (1996)

•United States Department of Justice. Office of Justice Programs. Bureau of

Justice Statistics. National Crime Victimization Survey, 2010.

•Weisburd, D., & Telep, C.W. (2010). The efficiency of place based

policing. Journal of Police Studies. 17, 247-262.

•Werthman, C. and Piliavin, I. (1967). Gang Members and the Police. In The

Police: Six Sociolgical Essays. 56-98. New York: John Wiley and Sons,

Inc. Edited by David J. Bordua.

•Wilson, J.Q., and Kelling, G. (1982). Broken windows: The police and neighborhood safety.

Atlantic Monthly (March), pp. 29-38.

•Wilson, O.W. (1963). Police Administration. 2nd ed. New York: McGraw-

Hill.

•Wright and Decker (1997) Armed Robbers in Action: Stickups and Street

Culture. Northeastern University Press.

•Wright, J. and Rossi, P. (1986). Armed and Considered Dangerous. A

Survey of Felons and Their Firearms.

www.ingramcontent.com/pod-product-compliance
Lightning Source LLC
Chambersburg PA
CBHW070549290526
45790CB00002B/608